POEMS

BY

A. D. HOPE

POEMS

BY

A. D. HOPE

NEW YORK THE VIKING PRESS 1961

Published in 1961 by The Viking Press, Inc.
625 Madison Avenue, New York 22, N.Y.

Library of Congress catalog card number : 61–17836

Printed in Great Britain by
WESTERN PRINTING SERVICES LTD BRISTOL

TO
AUDREY BEECHAM

Grateful acknowledgements are made to Messrs. Edwards and Shaw of Sydney who published the poet's first book, *The Wandering Islands*, in Australia, and have kindly consented to the reprinting of the following poems from their volume:

The Muse, The Pleasure of Princes, The Trophy, Pyramis or The House of Ascent, The Death of the Bird, Circe, Imperial Adam, Lot and his Daughters—I and II, The Return of Persephone, The Lamp and the Jar, The Gateway, Chorale, William Butler Yeats, Invocation, Flower Poem, Easter Hymn, The Wandering Islands, Ascent into Hell, Three Romances—I, II and III, Rawhead and Bloody Bones, The Dinner, Standardisation, The House of God, The Brides, Conquistador.

CONTENTS

PART ONE

PART ONE

SOLEDADES OF THE SUN
AND MOON

For P. K. Page

Now the year walks among the signs of heaven,
Swinging her large hips, smiling in all her motions,
Crosses with dancing steps the Milky Valley.
Round her the primal energies rejoice;
All the twelve metaphysical creatures and the seven
Swift spheres adore her vigour; the five oceans
   Look up and hear her voice
Ring through the ebony vault, where Ara Celi
Flames, and the choiring stars at their devotions
   With pure and jubilant noise
Praise and proclaim four seasons in her belly.

Four glittering worms, they sleep curled up inside her,
The unborn children of our isolation.
Solstice or song, in swift pursuit forever
We grieve in separate festivals of light.
What winged stallion, what immortal rider
Forks those wild flanks? What milk of generation
   Fills at a thrust the bright
Throat of the womb? By what supreme endeavour
Do the chaste Muses still take inspiration
   And tune the strings aright
By the god's bow that twangs to slay and sever?

Aimer of pestilence, Lucifer of healing,
Destroyer of the piping faun, Apollo!
Join these divided hearts. In single chorus
The raving sybil and the lucid seer
Find words to the one music, each revealing
Light in the other's dark, dark in that shining, hollow
   Galactic hemisphere

3

Which spins the changeless images before us.
Sign after sign, the constellations follow,
  Mirrored across the year
Where Scorpio views her house of death in Taurus.

Where the Wise Archer hangs his glittering quiver
Each son of Leda greets a heavenly brother.
As country or sex or song or birth conspire
The hemispheres set their crystal walls between.
Narcissus in air, Narcissus in the river
Drown in an alien element, or smother
  The lives towards which they lean.
Yet, through the burning circles of desire,
Immortal spirits behold, each in the other:
  His pillar of flame serene,
She, the unknown somnambulist of her fire.

Cradles of earth receive the salamander
But once at most in any generation;
Once in an age a desert tribe surprises
The solitary bird, the burning tree;
Innocent of their state, the poets wander,
Seeking the kindred of their incarnation,
  Waste land and homeless sea.
Phosphor declining as Orion rises
May for a brief hour break his isolation,
  The dying Phoenix see
New Phoenix blazing in her nest of spices.

Only in space, not time, the pattern changes:
Over your land of memory, enchanted
Glides the Celestial Swan, and in your bitter
Darkness the She-Bear shambles round the Pole;
Anvils of summer, in mine, the iron ranges
Rise from its arid heart to see the haunted
  River of Light unroll
Towards Achernar, where Hermes, the transmitter

Of spirits, herald of men and gods, has granted
   Speech between soul and soul,
And each to each the Swan and Phoenix glitter.

The mortal hearts of poets first engender
The parleying of those immortal creatures;
Then from their interchange create unending
Orbits of song and colloquies of light;
Sexes in their apocalyptic splendour
In mutual contemplation of their natures
   Transfigure or unite;
Descant and burden in diapason blending,
Urania dances, and the sacred gestures
   Become the words we write,
My lark arising or your dove descending.

For you the gods of song forgo their quarrel;
Panther and Wolf forget their former anger;
For you this ancient ceremony of greeting
Becomes a solemn apopemptic hymn.
Muses who twine the ivy with the laurel
In savage measures celebrate you, Stranger;
   For you the Maenads trim
Their torches and, in order due repeating
The stately ode, invoke you. Wanderer, Ranger,
   Beyond the utmost rim
Of waters, hear the voice of these entreating!

And, as the solitary bird of passage,
Loosing her heart across the wastes of ocean,
Sees round the cliffs of home the black tide crawling,
Accept the incantation of this verse;
Read its plain words; divine the secret message
By which the dance itself reveals a notion
   That moves our universe.
In the star rising or the lost leaf falling

5

The life of poetry, this enchanted motion,
    Perpetually recurs.
Take, then, this homage of our craft and calling!

Put on your figures of fable: with the chalice
From which the poets alone drink wisdom, healing
And joy that weds the thyrsus with the lyre,
Be Circe—or be my Queen of Sheba; come
Silent at nightfall to my silent palace
And read my heart, and rest; and when the wheeling
    Signs of the sky turn home,
I shall arise and show you in his byre
Among your milk-white dromedaries kneeling,
    Fierce in that lilied gloom,
My horn of gold, my unicorn of fire.

THE COASTS OF CERIGO

Half of the land, conscious of love and grief,
Half of the sea, cold creatures of the foam,
Mermaids still haunt and sing among the coves.
Sailors, who catch them basking on the reef,
Say they make love like women, and that some
Will die if once deserted by their loves.

Off shore, in deeper water, where the swell
Smokes round their crests, the cliffs of coral plunge
Fathom by fathom to the ocean floor.
There, rooted to the ooze-bed, as they tell,
Strange sister to the polyp and the sponge,
To holothurian and madrepore,

The Labra wallows in her bath of time
And, drowned in timeless sleep, displays the full
Grace of a goddess risen from the wave.
Small scarlet-crabs with awkward gestures climb
Through the black sea-weed drifting from her skull.
Her ladylegs gape darkly as a cave,

And through the coral clefts a gleam and gloom
Reveal the fronded arch, the pelvic gate;
Spotted and barred, the amorous fish swim in.
But in that hollow, mocking catacomb
Their love-songs echo and reverberate
A senseless clamour and a wordless din.

The love-trap closes on its gullible prey
Despite their sobs, despite their ecstasies.
Brilliant with tropic bands and stripes, they dart
Through a delicious juice which eats away
Their scales and soon dissolves their goggle eyes
And melts the milt-sac and the pulsing heart.

The divers on these coasts have cruel hands;
Their lives are hard; they do not make old bones;
The brutal masters send them down too deep.
But sometimes, as he combs the clefts and sands,
Among the oyster-beds and bearded stones
One comes upon the Labra fast asleep

And throws away his knife, his bag of pearl,
To take her in his arms and wrench her free.
Their bodies cling together as they rise
Spinning and drifting in the ocean swirl.
The seamen haul them in and stand to see
The exquisite, fabled creature as she dies.

But while in air they watch her choke and drown,
Enchanted by her beauty, they forget
The body of their comrade at her side,
From whose crushed lungs the bright blood oozing down
Jewel by ruby jewel from the wet
Deck drops and merges in the turquoise tide.

THE MUSE

She is Arachne. Instinct spins the net
Of her ferocious purpose in the night.
On her bared nerves the dew shakes bright and wet;
The angry goddess still with light
Tortures the web; for there the spider hangs
In loveliness no wisdom could invent
And conscious of the poison in her fangs.

She is Ariadne by the shore
Watching a black sail vanish on the sea,
While he, whose steps beyond the dreadful door
Were guided, and again set free,
The loutish prince forgets the path he trod;
And she, though she remembers, will consent
Soon to be tumbled by the drunken god.

She is Penelope. Nightlong at the loom
She must unravel the promise in her heart,
Subdue the monthly protest of the womb;
And still she knows, for all her art,
While its one poor design grows out of date,
The gods, who have all time, too late relent
And when her triumph comes, it comes too late.

To James McAuley, January 1945

THE PLEASURE OF PRINCES

What pleasures have great princes? These: to know
Themselves reputed mad with pride or power;
To speak few words—few words and short bring low
This ancient house, that city with flame devour;

To make old men, their fathers' enemies,
Drunk on the vintage of the former age;
To have great painters show their mistresses
Naked to the succeeding time; engage

The cunning of able, treacherous ministers
To serve, despite themselves, the cause they hate,
And leave a prosperous kingdom to their heirs
Nursed by the caterpillars of the state;

To keep their spies in good men's hearts; to read
The malice of the wise, and act betimes;
To hear the Grand Remonstrances of greed,
Led by the pure; cheat justice of her crimes;

To beget worthless sons and, being old,
By starlight climb the battlements, and while
The pacing sentry hugs himself for cold,
Keep vigil like a lover, muse and smile,

And think, to see from the grim castle steep
The midnight city below rejoice and shine:
'There my great demon grumbles in his sleep
And dreams of his destruction, and of mine.'

THE TROPHY

This the builder cannot guess,
Nor the lover's utmost skill:
In the instant of success
Suddenly the heart stands still;

Suddenly a shadow falls
On the builder's finished plan,
And the cry of love appals
All the energies of man.

What dire symbol of the heart
Comes, then, from its ancient tomb?
Image both of love and art,
See the Roman soldier come!

What great captain breaks his rest
All the annals cannot tell—
Stone lies blank upon his breast;
Bitter laurel shades him well—

What great captain's rigid will
Checked in flight his rabble host,
Roused them, drove them, cheered them still,
Though they knew the battle lost;

And, when the campaign was won
By the single force of pride,
Heard the ghost within him groan,
Fell upon his sword and died.

PYRAMIS *OR* THE HOUSE
OF ASCENT

This is their image: the desert and the wild,
A lone man digging, a nation piling stones
Under the lash in fear, in sweat, in haste;
Image of those demonic minds who build
To outlast time, spend life to house old bones—
This pyramid rising squarely in the waste!

I think of the great work, its secret lost;
The solid, blind, invincible masonry
Still challenges the heart. Neglect and greed
Have left it void and ruin; sun and frost
Fret it away; yet, all foretold, I see
The builder answering: 'Let the work proceed!'

I think of how the work was hurried on:
Those terrible souls, the Pharaohs, those great Kings
Taking, like genius, their prerogative
Of blood, mind, treasure: 'Tomorrow I shall be gone;
If you lack slaves, make war! The measure of things
Is man, and I of men. By this you live.'

No act of time limits the procreant will
And to subdue men seems a little thing,
Seeing that in another world than this
The gods themselves unwilling await him still
And must be overcome; for thus the King
Takes, for all men, his apotheosis.

I think of other pyramids, not in stone,
The great, incredible monuments of art,
And of their builders, men who put aside

Consideration, dared, and stood alone,
Strengthening those powers that fence the failing heart:
Intemperate will and incorruptible pride.

The man alone digging his bones a hole;
The pyramid in the waste—whose images?
Blake's tower of vision defying the black air;
Milton twice blind groping about his soul
For exit, and Swift raving mad in his—
The builders of the pyramid everywhere!

THE DEATH OF THE BIRD

For every bird there is this last migration:
Once more the cooling year kindles her heart;
With a warm passage to the summer station
Love pricks the course in lights across the chart.

Year after year a speck on the map, divided
By a whole hemisphere, summons her to come;
Season after season, sure and safely guided,
Going away she is also coming home.

And being home, memory becomes a passion
With which she feeds her brood and straws her nest,
Aware of ghosts that haunt the heart's possession
And exiled love mourning within the breast.

The sands are green with a mirage of valleys;
The palm-tree casts a shadow not its own;
Down the long architrave of temple or palace
Blows a cool air from moorland scarps of stone.

And day by day the whisper of love grows stronger;
That delicate voice, more urgent with despair,
Custom and fear constraining her no longer,
Drives her at last on the waste leagues of air.

A vanishing speck in those inane dominions,
Single and frail, uncertain of her place,
Alone in the bright host of her companions,
Lost in the blue unfriendliness of space,

She feels it close now, the appointed season:
The invisible thread is broken as she flies;
Suddenly, without warning, without reason,
The guiding spark of instinct winks and dies.

14

Try as she will, the trackless world delivers
No way, the wilderness of light no sign,
The immense and complex map of hills and rivers
Mocks her small wisdom with its vast design.

And darkness rises from the eastern valleys,
And the winds buffet her with their hungry breath,
And the great earth, with neither grief nor malice,
Receives the tiny burden of her death.

CIRCE

after the painting by Dosso Dossi

Behind her not the quivering of a leaf
Flutters the deep enchantment of the wood;
No ripple at her feet disturbs the well;
She sits among her lovers dazed with grief,
Bewildered by the charge of alien blood.
Herself transfigured by the hideous spell

She sits among her creatures motionless,
Sees the last human shadow of despair
Fade from the sad, inquisitive, animal eyes,
The naked body of the sorceress
Mocked by the light, sleek shapes of feather and hair.
And as on snout and beak and muzzle dies

The melancholy trace of human speech,
For the first time her heart is rich with words
And with her voice she disenchants the grove.
The lonely island and the sounding beach
Answer with barks and howls, the scream of birds,
Her uncontrollable, aching cry of love.

PASIPHAE

There stood the mimic cow; the young bull kept
Fast by the nose-ring, trampling in his pride,
Nuzzled her flanks and snuffed her naked side.
She was a queen: to have her will she crept
In that black box; and when her lover leapt
And fell thundering on his wooden bride,
When straight her fierce, frail body crouched inside
Felt the wet pizzle pierce and plunge, she wept.

She wept for terror, for triumph; she wept to know
Her love unable to embrace its bliss
So long imagined, waking and asleep.
But when within she felt the pulse, the blow,
The burst of copious seed, the burning kiss
Fill her with monstrous life, she did not weep.

IMPERIAL ADAM

Imperial Adam, naked in the dew,
Felt his brown flanks and found the rib was gone.
Puzzled he turned and saw where, two and two,
The mighty spoor of Jahweh marked the lawn.

Then he remembered through mysterious sleep
The surgeon fingers probing at the bone,
The voice so far away, so rich and deep:
'It is not good for him to live alone.'

Turning once more he found Man's counterpart
In tender parody breathing at his side.
He knew her at first sight, he knew by heart
Her allegory of sense unsatisfied.

The pawpaw drooped its golden breasts above
Less generous than the honey of her flesh;
The innocent sunlight showed the place of love;
The dew on its dark hairs winked crisp and fresh.

This plump gourd severed from his virile root,
She promised on the turf of Paradise
Delicious pulp of the forbidden fruit;
Sly as the snake she loosed her sinuous thighs,

And waking, smiled up at him from the grass;
Her breasts rose softly and he heard her sigh—
From all the beasts whose pleasant task it was
In Eden to increase and multiply

Adam had learned the jolly deed of kind:
He took her in his arms and there and then,
Like the clean beasts, embracing from behind,
Began in joy to found the breed of men.

Then from the spurt of seed within her broke
Her terrible and triumphant female cry,
Split upward by the sexual lightning stroke.
It was the beasts now who stood watching by:

The gravid elephant, the calving hind,
The breeding bitch, the she-ape big with young
Were the first gentle midwives of mankind;
The teeming lioness rasped her with her tongue;

The proud vicuña nuzzled her as she slept
Lax on the grass; and Adam watching too
Saw how her dumb breasts at their ripening wept,
The great pod of her belly swelled and grew,

And saw its water break, and saw, in fear,
Its quaking muscles in the act of birth,
Between her legs a pigmy face appear,
And the first murderer lay upon the earth.

LOT AND HIS DAUGHTERS—I

The ruddy fire-glow, like her sister's eyes,
Flickered on her bare breasts and licked along
The ripeness of her savage flanks; a tongue
Of darkness curled between her restless thighs.

Black as the Syrian night, on her young head
Clustered the tendrils of their ancient vine;
The cave gaped with its drunken mouth; the wine
Babbled, unceasing, from the old man's bed:

'I have two daughters . . . let them serve your need
. . . virgins . . . but these, my guests . . . you understand'—
She crept in and lay down. Her Promised Land
Lay waiting for the sower with his seed.

She felt him stir; she felt herself embraced;
The tough old arms bit hard on loin and breast;
The great beard smothered her. She was possessed.
A lioness roared abruptly in the waste.

But Lot's grim heart was far away. Beside
The Jordan stream, in other days, he stood
And kept the great beast, raging, from her brood,
And drove his javelin through her tawny hide.

LOT AND HIS DAUGHTERS—II

The sun above the hills raged in the height.
Within Lot's cave, his vine-stock's living screen
Filtered the noon-day glare to a dim green
And hung the fat grapes bunched against the light.

The rascal patriarch, the bad old man,
Naked and rollicking on his heap of straw,
Scratching his hairy cods—one drunken paw
Spilled the red liquor from its silver can.

His beard, white as a blossoming branch, gaped wide;
Out flew a laugh: 'By God, the wine is out!
More wine!'
　　　The cavern rumbled to his shout.
Brown fingers pushed the leafy screen aside.

And, padding broadly with their bare-foot tread,
Calm-eyed, big-bellied, purposeful and slow,
Lot's delicate daughters, in the bloom and glow
Of their fulfilment stood beside his bed.

Crafty from fear, reckless with joy and greed,
The old man held them in his crapulous eye:
Mountains of promise bulging in his sky;
Ark of his race; God's covenant to his seed.

They stooped to take his cup, tilted and poured;
The must rose mantling to the glittering rim;
And, as the heart of Lot grew bold in him,
It boasted and exulted in the Lord.

'The one Just Man from Sodom saved alive!
Did not His finger point me to this cave?
Behold His hand once more stretched out to save!
For Jahweh too is just. My seed shall thrive.

'Shall not the Judge of all the earth do right?
Why did his angels take me by the hand?
My tribe shall yet be numbered with the sand
Upon the shore and with the stars of night.

'With me it shall be as with Abraham.
Dark are His ways, but sure and swift to bless—
How should my ewes breed in the wilderness?
And lo, the Lord himself provides a ram!'

But Lot's resourceful daughters, side by side,
Smiled back, inscrutable, patient and content;
Their slender bodies, ripe and eloquent,
Swayed like the standing corn at harvest-tide.

And, conscious of what trouble stirred below
His words and flickered in his shrewd old eyes,
They placed the cup that kept their father wise
In that best wisdom, which is not to know.

THE RETURN OF PERSEPHONE

Gliding through the still air, he made no sound;
Wing-shod and deft, dropped almost at her feet,
And searched the ghostly regiments and found
The living eyes, the tremor of breath, the beat
Of blood in all that bodiless underground.

She left her majesty; she loosed the zone
Of darkness and put by the rod of dread.
Standing, she turned her back upon the throne
Where, well she knew, the Ruler of the Dead,
Lord of her body and being, sat like stone;

Stared with his ravenous eyes to see her shake
The midnight drifting from her loosened hair,
The girl once more in all her actions wake,
The blush of colour in her cheeks appear
Lost with her flowers that day besides the lake.

The summer flowers scattering, the shout,
The black manes plunging down to the black pit—
Memory or dream? She stood awhile in doubt,
Then touched the Traveller God's brown arm and met
His cool, bright glance and heard his words ring out:

'Queen of the Dead and Mistress of the Year!'
—His voice was the ripe ripple of the corn;
The touch of dew, the rush of morning air—
'Remember now the world where you were born;
The month of your return at last is here.'

And still she did not speak, but turned again
Looking for answer, for anger, for command:
The eyes of Dis were shut upon their pain;
Calm as his marble brow, the marble hand
Slept on his knee. Insuperable disdain

Foreknowing all bounds of passion, of power, of art,
Mastered but could not mask his deep despair.
Even as she turned with Hermes to depart,
Looking her last on her grim ravisher
For the first time she loved him from her heart.

THE LAMP AND THE JAR

You are that vessel full of holy oil:
Wisdom, unstirring in its liquid sleep,
Hoarded and cool, lucid and golden green,
Fills the pure flanks of the containing stone;
Here darkness mellows what the sunlit soil
To purposes unknown, for ends unseen,
Produced, and labour of unnumbered men.
All the unthinking earth with fret or toil
Reared, ripened, buried in the earth again,
Here lives, and living, waits: this source alone
Distils those fruitful tears the Muses weep.

And I, the lamp before the sacred ark,
The root of fire, the burning flower of light,
Draw from your loins this inexhaustible joy.
There the perpetual miracle of grace
Recurs, as, from its agony, the flame
Feeds the blind heart of the adoring dark;
And there the figures of our mystery,
The shapes of terror and inhuman woe,
Emerge and prophesy; there with the mark
Of blood upon his breast and on his brow,
An unknown king, with my transfigured face,
Bends your immortal body to his delight.

THE GATEWAY

Now the heart sings with all its thousand voices
To hear this city of cells, my body, sing.
The tree through the stiff clay at long last forces
Its thin strong roots and taps the secret spring.

And the sweet waters without intermission
Climb to the tips of its green tenement;
The breasts have borne the grace of their possession,
The lips have felt the pressure of content.

Here I come home: in this expected country
They know my name and speak it with delight.
I am the dream and you my gates of entry,
The means by which I waken into light.

CHORALE

Often had I found her fair;
Most when to my bed she came,
Naked as the moving air,
Slender, walking like a flame.
In that grace I sink and drown:
Opening like the liquid wave
To my touch she laid her down,
Drew me to her crystal cave.
  Love me ever, love me long—
  Was the burden of her song.

All divisions vanish there;
Now her eyes grow dark and still;
Now I feel the living air
With contending thunder fill;
Hear the shuddering cry begin,
Feel the heart leap in her breast,
And her moving loins within
Clasp their strong, rejoicing guest.
  Love me now, O now, O long!
  Is the burden of her song.

Now the wave recedes and dies;
Dancing fires descend the hill;
Blessed spirits from our eyes
Gaze in wonder and are still.
Yes our wondering spirits come
From their timeless anguish freed:
Yet within they hear the womb
Sighing for the wasted seed.
  Love may not delay too long—
  Is the burden of their song.

WILLIAM BUTLER YEATS

To have found at last that noble, candid speech
In which all things worth saying may be said,
Which, whether the mind asks, or the heart bids, to each
Affords its daily bread;

To have been afraid neither of lust nor hate,
To have shown the dance, and when the dancer ceased,
The bloody head of prophecy on a plate
Borne in at Herod's feast;

To have loved the bitter, lucid mind of Swift,
Bred passion against the times, made wisdom strong;
To have sweetened with your pride's instinctive gift
The brutal mouth of song;

To have shared with Blake uncompromising scorn
For art grown smug and clever, shown your age
The virgin leading home the unicorn
And loosed his sacred rage—

But more than all, when from my arms she went
That blessed my body all night, naked and near,
And all was done, and order and content
Closed the Platonic Year,

Was it *not* chance alone that made us look
Into the glass of the Great Memory
And know the eternal moments, in your book,
That we had grown to be?

INVOCATION

*To the gods all things are fair and good and right, but men
hold some things wrong and some right.*

HERAKLEITOS. FR. 61

You near, you watchful, you invisible one
In whom all just desires arise and end,
Inscrutable presence, guide, deliverer, friend,
Whose will against my will, at need, is done!

In the great dark behind me I see well
Purpose, beyond my purpose, draw me here.
Towards what end? Now, in my fortieth year,
I look into the light and cannot tell.

Little by little a wisdom that I lacked
Grows in this heart, to see and know your sign;
But not the habit of courage that should be mine:
Damnation still hangs on that naked act

By which the few, the free, the chosen light
Our way, and deeply live and proudly move,
Renew the uncompromising choice of love,
Engender power and beauty on our night.

That breed is in my bones: in me again
The spirit elect works out its mighty plan—
Yes, but that birth is hard. In the grown man
Habit corrupts the will with terror or pain.

My passion, my gift, my vision can I betray?
Must for my pride the innocent be undone?
How shall I act? My dangerous days come on;
The lion and the dragon fill each way.

For, if I do the dragon's will, I see
Custom is served—and I am lost indeed.
But in the lion's burning eyes I read
Unjust, severe, divine Necessity

Declare her law. Unmoved upon her hill
She guards the eternal measures of the world;
But at the laws of men her lip is curled,
The frantic devotees of good and ill.

All perish in the Herakleitan fire;
But grace and mastery are in her hand
And she grants those, who learn and understand,
Vision that crowns the might of their desire.

Then, as the poets, who alone defend
That darkness out of which our light is won,
Strengthen my love—but flash no beam upon
The future; show the meaning, not the end!

Lest the mind, knowing too well the things to be,
Lose its blind courage and forget its part,
And no more trust its lightnings, nor the heart
Kindle and quicken at the mystery.

AN EPISTLE

EDWARD SACKVILLE TO VENETIA DIGBY

Ainsi, bruyante abeille, au retour du matin,
Je vois changer en miel les délices du thym.

First, last and always dearest, closest, best,
   Source of my travail and my rest,
The letter which I shall not send, I write
   To cheer my more than arctic night.
Sole day and all my summer in that year
   Of darkness, you were here,
Were here but yesterday, and still I go
   Rapt in its golden afterglow.
Caught in the webs of memory and desire,
   The cooling and the kindling fire,
Through all this house, from room to room I pace:
   Here at the stair we met; this place
You sat in; still I see you sitting there,
   As though some trace the printless air
Retained; a tremulous hush, as though you spoke,
   Enchants its silence; here your cloak
I held for you and here you looked farewell
   And went, but did not break the spell,
By which I feel you here yet know you gone—
   So men, who winking see the sun
And turn into the dark, awhile descry
   His image on the dazzled eye.
But like a tale I tell it all again
   And gloss it with a scholar's pen,
For so Love, though he harvest all his store,
   Gleans in bare fields to make it more.
Now like the garner ant when frosts begin,
   I have my harvest heaped within:
Abundance for my year to come, a feast
   Still cherished, still increased;

For all it spends from its ripe yesterday
  The heart shall copiously repay:
Words, glances, motions, all that I rehearse
  My joy transfigures, as great verse
From music may have a perfection lent
  More than the poet knew or meant;
And as the cunning craftsman can prolong
  Through cadences and shifts of song,
And make what was by nature beautiful,
  By art more dulcet, keen and full,
So from one day, one meeting, I prepare
  Music to last me out the year.

Yet I cannot recall it as I should;
  Too much surprised by joy I stood,
A child who finds his long expected treat,
  Coming, too sudden and too sweet—
Or greedily I gulped it like a beast
  And missed the true, the lasting taste.

'Poor beast,' I say, 'poor beast indeed, who comes
  To be content with scraps and crumbs!
Poor heart, poor Lazarus, overjoyed to wait
  The scrapings of another's plate!'
For, though I could restore, vivid and strong,
  That late, pure, breathless trance of song,
I know myself but a dumb listener, where
  I have sung bourdon to her air.

I that was rich, now at the treasury door
  May only glimpse that golden store
Piled in fantastic heaps; the jewelled shrine
  Worship, not touch, no longer mine;
At most, a starveling Tantalus, must see
  The shadow crop upon my tree
Slide through the hand and from my gaping lip
  The mocking naiad glide and slip.

Or rather—for in similes of woe
  I lose my way—full well I know
The food was real: 'Twas I who could not eat
  The spirit's insubstantial meat,
Pleasure of angels, such as flesh and blood
  Taste not, though all may take their food.
I, who have held you in my human arms,
  Must gaze as if on ghostly charms,
Or on the painting of a mistress dead—
  Yet we both breathe and might to bed.
To bed! At the mere thought I feel arise
  That rebel in the flesh, who cries:
'It was no picture we saw yesterday,
  But she, in all the living play
Of light on restless body, limbs, hair, breast,
  Eyes, hands—what need to tell the rest?'
What need? But, ah, what sure recourse of joy!
  This nothing can or shall destroy,
Custom deny nor honour stand between,
  Nor your own change of heart demean.
He whose you are, your husband and my friend
  —I do not grudge it, but commend—
Took, when he took you hence, your picture too
  Lest I should keep some part in you.

What should I care, who had my gallery lined,
  Crowded with pictures of the mind?
What care for silk or lute string who possess
  The splendour of your nakedness,
The lily, the jet, the coral and the rose
  Varied in pleasure and repose?
Three years we lived as blessed angels do
  Who to each other show the true
Bareness of spirit and, only when they would
  Travel abroad, wear flesh and blood.
So clothed we met the world: at set of sun,
  Our foolish, needful business done,

Home we would turn, eager to taste at even
  Our native and our naked heaven.
So now by heart each single grace and all
  Their glowing postures I recall.
Absent, you come unbidden; present, you
  Walk naked to my naked view;
Dead, I could resurrect you from your dust;
  So exquisite, individual, just
The bare, bright flesh, I swear my eyes could tell
  You by throat, thighs or breast as well,
Or any least part almost, as your face.

    Alas, as courtiers out of place
Speak of the court, I boast and dream the rest.
  In exile now and dispossessed
I think of how we used, so long ago,
  In that tremendous overthrow
Of our first worlds, when first we loved, first knew
  No world except these selves, this Two,
How we would laugh to see that Last World pass
  For real beyond our Wall of Glass;
And we untouched, untouchable, serene,
  Plighted within our magic screen,
Would pity those without, whose curious eyes
  Could see, could judge, could recognise,
Know with the mind, but coldly and in part,
  Not with the comprehending heart.
This was our game; and, with the growth of love,
  We said, these walls of glass remove;
We re-embody those shadows by our joy;
  The frontiers of desire deploy
Until our latitudes of grace extend
  Round the great globe and bend
Back on themselves, to end where we begin
  Love's wars that take the whole world in.
So little states, rich in great men and sound
  In arts and virtues, gather ground

And grow to empires mighty in their day.
    And we, we said, more blest than they,
Shall not decline as Persian kingdoms do
    Or those the Tartar overthrew.
Who lives outside our universal state?
    And all within ourselves create.
Will angels fall twice, or the moon breed Turks?
    Or dread we our own works?—
But even while the architects designed
    The finials, their towers were mined.
He, your child-lover, twice reported dead,
    Once false—but all was false—some said
He died at Pont-de-Cé, and some said not
    But on rough alps his bones might rot—
For whom, though your heart grieved, it grieved as for
    Childhood itself that comes no more,
Yet came, and not as ghosts come from the grave,
    But as strong spirits come to save,
And claimed the love we buried long ago.
    I watched it rise and live. I know,
Alas, I know, though I believed it not,
    The spell he casts who breaks the knot;
And this you told me once and bade me learn
    Even before his strange return.

Now it is I outside our Wall. I stand
    And once a year may kiss that hand
Which once with my whole body of man made free—
    O, my twice-lost Eurydice,
Twice must I make my journey down to Hell,
    Twice its grim gods by prayer compel,
And twice, to win you only for a day,
    The spirit's bitter reckoning pay,
Yet for my first default their just decree
    Grants me to hear you now and see,
As deserts know peace, as barren waters calms,
    Only forbidding me your arms.

Why, since my case is hopeless, do I still
   Exacerbate this wrench of will
Against the force of reason, honour, rest
   And all that is in manhood best?
Is not this second Orpheus worse than he
   Who perished in his misery,
Torn by the drunken women in their chase
   Among the echoing hills of Thrace?
To cherish and prolong the state I loathe
   Am I not drunk or mad or both?

Not so! These torments mind and heart approve,
   And are the sacrifice of love.
The soul sitting apart sees what I do,
   Who win powers more than Orpheus knew,
Though he tamed tigers and enchanted trees
   And broached the chthonic mysteries.
The gate beyond the gate that I found fast
   Has opened to your touch at last.
Nothing is lost for those who pass this door:
   They contemplate their world before
And in the carcase of the lion come
   Upon the unguessed honeycomb.
There are no words for this new happiness,
   But such as fables may express.
Fabling I tell it then as best I can:
   That pre-diluvian age of man
Most like had mighty poets, even as ours,
   Or grant them nobler themes and powers.
When Nature fashioned giants in the dew
   Surely the morning Muses too
Created genius in an ampler mould
   To celebrate her Age of Gold.
Yet think, for lack of letters all was lost,
   Think Homer's *Iliads* to our cost
Gone like those epics from before the Flood
   As, but for Cadmus, sure they would.

Books now preserve for us the boasts of time;
  But what preserved them in the Prime?
Where did they live, those royal poems then,
  But in the hearts and mouths of men,
Men of no special genius, talents, parts,
  Patience their sole gift, all their arts
Memory, the nurse, not mother, of ancient songs;
  No seraph from God's fire with tongs
Took the live coal and laid it on their lips;
  And yet, until their last eclipse,
Age after age, those giant harmonies
  Lodged in such brains, as birds in trees.
The music of the spheres, which no man's wit
  Conceives, once heard, he may transmit:
Love was that music, and by love indeed
  We serve the greater nature's need.
As on the rough back of some stream in flood
  Whose current is by rocks withstood,
We see in all that ruin and rush endure
  A form miraculously pure;
A standing wave through which the waters race
  Yet keeps its crystal shape and place,
So shapes and creatures of eternity
  We form or bear. Though more than we,
Their substance and their being we sustain
  Awhile, though they, not we, remain.
And, still, while we have part in them, we can
  Surpass the single reach of man,
Put on strange powers and vision we knew not of—
  And thus it has been with my love.
Fresh modes of being, unguessed forms of bliss
  Have been, are mine: But more than this,
Our bodies, aching in their blind embrace,
  Once thought they touched the pitch of grace.
Made for that end alone, in their delight,
  They thought that single act and rite
Paid nature's debt and heaven's. Even so
  There was a thing they could not know:

Nature, who makes each member to one end,
    May give it powers which transcend
Its first and fruitful purpose. When she made
    The Tongue for taste, who in the shade
Of summer vines, what speechless manlike brute,
    Biting sharp rind or sweeter fruit,
Could have conceived the improbable tale, the long
    Strange fable of the Speaking Tongue?
So Love, which Nature's craft at first designed
    For comfort and increase of kind,
Puts on another nature, grows to be
    The language of the mystery;
The heart resolves its chaos then, the soul
    Lucidly contemplates the whole
Just order of the random world; and through
    That dance she moves, and dances too.

THE TOMB OF PENTHESILEA

The Hero's tomb is gone;
Yet here beside,
A solitary stone
Speaks for the Hero's bride.
Trace, Traveller, with the tried
And dusty staff
Her epitaph:

'Stranger, here rusts the bright
Bare weapon won,
That day he faced in fight
The brutish horde alone,
And took from an unknown
Adversary
The wound, and me.

'The man who masters men,
Knows but his star.
Love must complete him then;
He learns from sword and scar
The purpose of his war,
And with firm tread
Tramps on the dead.

'In pride he drew his breath
Who mastered me:
So glorious the sheathe,
That jewelled panoply,
How splendid then must be
The soul, the thin
True blade within!

'It was my pride to lie
And lightly press
Against a marching thigh;
To have his hand embrace
My armature of grace;
To watch, to keep
His helpless sleep;

'To flash in the loud war
On flesh; to feel
The bitter life-blood pour
Raging along the steel;
To know, and to conceal
My gift to know
His final foe;

'To triumph then in fate—
The great hour come,
The blade spoke out elate;
The hidden wound was dumb.
He knew, as death struck home,
In that, in this
Lay the sword's bliss.'

MEDITATION ON A BONE

A piece of bone, found at Trondhjem in 1901, with the following runic inscription (about A.D. 1050) cut on it:

*I loved her as a maiden; I will not trouble Erlend's detestable wife;
better she should be a widow.*

Words scored upon a bone,
Scratched in despair or rage—
Nine hundred years have gone;
Now, in another age,
They burn with passion on
A scholar's tranquil page.

The scholar takes his pen
And turns the bone about,
And writes those words again.
Once more they seethe and shout,
And through a human brain
Undying hate rings out.

'I loved her when a maid;
I loathe and love the wife
That warms another's bed:
Let him beware his life!'
The scholar's hand is stayed;
His pen becomes a knife

To grave in living bone
The fierce archaic cry.
He sits and reads his own
Dull sum of misery.
A thousand years have flown
Before that ink is dry.

And, in a foreign tongue,
A man, who is not he,
Reads and his heart is wrung
This ancient grief to see,
And thinks: When I am dung,
What bone shall speak for me?

THE DREAM

Unable to speak, exhausted by the search,
He stood and stared his love and unbelief
For the incredible luck that brought them there;
The clatter and fury of the endless march
Now stilled, the whisper of his inward grief
Dripped on and filled the cave of his despair.

'Be quick! You have so little time,' she said;
'Listen! My terror stands breathing on the stair;
And soon you must go back into the storm.
Darling!' she said, and made her body bare
And drew him down beside her on the bed,
'See, you are cold; come to my heart, be warm!'

Unable to speak, he touched her with his hand,
Fingering the witnesses of cheek and breast.
The bloody anguish breeding in the bone
Told its long exile, told of all the lands
Where the unresting heart, seeking its rest,
Finds always that its language is unknown.

They knew in that fierce, shuddering first embrace,
Clearer than words, more desperate than a cry,
All that their spirits had borne and could not say:
Journeys that always led to the wrong place,
The maps whose promises turned out a lie,
The messages that always went astray.

There in each other's gaze they saw the vast
Deserts of sand where round them wheeled and swept
Voices of pleading or insane abuse;
A jungle of hands clutched at them as they passed
Breaking the fingers they could not unloose;
And eyes of malice watched them while they slept;

43

And golden bodies, counterfeiting love,
Won them with grace or pity—they woke to know
Mechanical, alien arms about them close,
The piston sliding in its greasy groove;
The masks of beauty fell aside, to show
An ulcer of pleasure eating away the nose,

The maggots writhing in a fly-blown eye—
There they lost hope, and the sane world forgot,
And nightmare grew at last to be their home.
Mysterious names were scrawled across the sky;
They tried to leave but found their passports not
In order, or the permit had not come;

And had set out at last alone, at night,
To be sent back: the frontier had been closed.
Clutching their parcels they were made to wait
For years in rooms blazing with too much light;
Were called for questioning or, while they dozed,
Wakened by blows and screaming at the gate.

Their names were shouted; they were led away.
The guards were friendly, but they did not know
The destination, or they would not tell;
In storm and terror and boredom, day by day
They struggled over passes deep with snow
Or plodded across deserts they knew too well.

Year after year the march went on: they grew
Accustomed to the noise, the dust, the chain,
The never being alone, the senseless haste
From nowhere to some end that no one knew.
They lay at night and heard the torrents of rain
Lashing the roofs, a fury of ruin and waste.

44

One day among the mountains, in the rough
Streets of a steep, unknown, unfriendly town,
Marching at dusk, the labouring columns met.
Their eyes held; they stood still; the chain dropped off;
They looked about them and they were alone;
She smiled and spoke his name; her eyes were wet.

Unable to speak, he touched her with his hand;
Unhurried and unafraid they moved away.
The doors stood wide; they climbed the silent stair.
There the room opened like their promised land.
Quiet as death he stood and watched the way
Her fingers moved as she let down her hair.

So close they lay; so cold, so fierce, so still
Their joy! Their dream so deep, so strong and full,
Folded them nearer and remade their world.
She felt her breasts against his breast, the thrill
Of his quick breath; he felt, at last, the dull
Beat of his blood, her arms about him curled;

And little by little she warmed him with her love;
The lineaments of grace, the gesture of peace,
Became their language, their enchanted speech,
Clothed her with courage and filled her body and drove
Away his guilt and gave his gift release;
And all their acts were answered, each to each.

She felt the frosty rigor that bound him turned
To ease—But the bright warmth she gave became
A fever of heat. In wonder and dismay
She felt him filled with fire; her flesh was burned
And from his mouth an unendurable flame
Scorched her, and she cried out and shrank away

45

And leapt up; for the bed was all alight—
Unable to speak, he rose and left her there;
Unable to meet her eyes that gazed with such
Anguish and horror, went out into the night,
Burning, burning, burning in her despair
And kindling hurt and ruin at his touch.

THE WALKER

'Who walks round my house all night?
None but lanky Tom.'
AN OLD CHILDREN'S GAME

Who walks round my house all night,
Stepping sad and slow,
Ghost or woman, child or sprite?
None that I do know.

Who is she that haunts the dark
When the moon is down,
Street or garden, pale or park,
Through the sleeping town?

When the frost falls thick and chill
And the stars slide by,
In my bed I hear it still,
Hear her walk and sigh.

Sultry midnights when I wake
In the clutch of fear,
Though my bones with fever shake,
Nothing do I hear;

Nothing, nothing can I spy
Through the darkened pane;
Yet, when on my bed I lie,
Come those steps again;

Comes the sound of mortal grief
And the tread of woe—
Is it woman, spirit, thief,
Pacing to and fro?

47

'Lover, keep your careless bed,
Turn you to the wall.
Not the living, not the dead
Answers here your call;

'But a witness from the void,
Banned with drug and knife,
Whom your coward heart destroyed
In the gates of life.'

LAST LOOK

His mind, as he was going out of it,
Looked emptier, shabbier than it used to be:
A secret look to which he had no key,
Something misplaced, something that did not fit.

Windows without their curtains seemed to stare
Inward—but surely once they had looked out.
Someone had moved the furniture about
And changed the photographs: the frames were there,

But idiot faces never seen before
Leered back at him. He knew there should have been
A carpet on the boards, not these obscene
Clusters of toadstools sprouting through the floor.

Yet Arabella's portrait on the wall
Followed him just as usual with its eyes.
Was it reproach or pleading, or surprise,
Or love perhaps, or something of them all?

Watching her lips, he saw them part; could just
Catch the thin sibilance of her concern:
'O Richard, Richard, why would you not learn
I was the only soul that you could trust?'

Carefully, carefully, seeming not to know,
He added this remembrance to his store.
Conscience, in uniform beside the door,
Coughed and remarked that it was time to go.

High time indeed! He heard their tramping feet.
To have stayed even so long, he knew, was rash.
The mob was in the house. He heard the crash
Of furniture hurled down into the street.

'This way!' the warder said; 'You must be quick.
You will be safe with us'—He turned to go
And saw too late the gaping void below.
Someone behind him laughed. A brutal kick

Caught him below the shoulders and he fell.
Quite slowly, clutching at the passing air,
He plunged towards the source of his despair
Down the smooth funnel of an endless well.

AN EPISTLE FROM HOLOFERNES

'Great Holofernes, Captain of the Host,
To Judith: Greeting! And, because his ghost
Neither forgets nor sleeps, peace to her heart!
He, being dead, would play a nobler part;
Yet, being a spirit unpacified, must seek
Vengeance. Take warning then; for souls that speak
Truth to the living, must be fed with blood.
Do not neglect his rites: give him that food
Without which ghosts are powerless to control
Malice which breeds by nature in the soul.
Take down the shining scimitar again;
Slay him with a cock, a kid to ease his pain.
For otherwise his talk is double talk,
And he must haunt you. Then, where'er you walk,
Hear his blood dripping from your bag of meat
And, at your table, sitting in your seat,
See the Great Captain's carcase; in your bed
Always upon your pillow grins the Head;
And bloodier whispers that infect the mind
Revenge in dreams the unacted deed of kind.
Think not the Jews nor the Jews' god shall save:
Charms are not sovereign beyond the grave,
And he who warns you, though he wish you well,
Has arms to take and hold you even in Hell.'
Thus in a fable once I spoke to you;
Now other times require I speak it new.
How easy it would be if this were all,
Dear, then the house might totter: it should not fall;
Then, we should utter with our living breath
A healing language from the mouths of death;
In Judith you, in Holofernes I
Might know our legend. But, in days gone by,
This would have been a magic rod whose blow
Broke the parched rocks and made their waters flow.

We should have certainty to conjure with,
Acting the saving ritual of our myth;
The earthquake over, the air sweet and still,
Take courage against this sickness of the will;
For when in former times the myths were true,
For every trouble there was a thing to do:
He, who in faith assumed his Hero's part,
Performed a solemn cleansing of the heart:
The lustral waters, spilling from the bowl,
Poured on the guilty hands and purged the soul;
And sacred dances acted as a spell
To set a lid upon the Hideous Well.
Myths formed the rituals by which ancient men
Groped towards the dayspring and were born again.
Now, though the myths still serve us in our need,
From fear and from desire we are not freed;
Nor can the helpless torment in the breast
Act out its own damnation and have rest.
Yet myth has other uses: it confirms
The heart's conjectures and approves its terms
Against the servile speech of compromise,
Habit which blinds, custom which overlies
And masks us from ourselves—the myths define
Our figure and motion in the Great Design,
Cancel the accidents of name and place,
Set the fact naked against naked space,
And speak to us the truth of what we are.
As overhead the frame of star and star
Still sets rejoicing on the midnight air
Orion's girdle, Berenice's hair,
So when we take our legend for a guide
The firmament of vision opens wide.
Against the sweep of dark and silence lie
Our constellations spread upon the sky.
Plain is the language of those glorious ones;
The meteors flash through their glittering bones;
Freed from the sun of custom, they describe

What, by the daylight vision of the tribe,
We felt, unseeing. We in the mythic night
Know our own motion, burn with our own light,
Study high calm and shining, scorn the more
The beast that winks and snuffles at the door.

Yet the myths will not fit us ready made.
It is the meaning of the poet's trade
To re-create the fables and revive
In men the energies by which they live,
To reap the ancient harvests, plant again
And gather in the visionary grain,
And to transform the same unchanging seed
Into the gospel-bread on which they feed.
But they who trust the fables over much
Lose the real world, plain sight and common touch,
And, in their mythopœic fetters bound,
Stand to be damned upon infernal ground,
Finding, no matter to what creed they look,
Half their salvation was not in the book.
Then books turn vampires and they drink our blood,
They who feed vampires join the vampire's brood
And, changed to hideous academic birds,
Eat living flesh and vomit it as words.
Our wills must re-imagine what they act
And in ourselves find what the fable lacked.
The myths indeed the Logos may impart,
But *verbum caro factum* is our part.
Thus, though our legend with its proving flame
Burns all to essence, shows in you the same
Temper of ancient virtue, force of will,
That saved the trembling people on the hill;
Though I myself in Holofernes know
Your bloody and greedy and insensate foe
And, at my feast, hear a relentless voice
Declare my grim dichotomy of choice:

53

Sound a retreat, or move to one event:
The headless carrion rolling in the tent;
Yet imaged new the fable is not plain:
Though Judith live and though the foe be slain,
Ours is a warfare of a different kind
Pitched in the unknown landscape of the mind,
Where both sides lose, yet both sides claim the day
And who besieges whom is hard to say;
Where each, by other foes encircled round,
Hears in the night far off the bubbling sound
Of the sweet springs that are to both denied,
And sees false watch-fires crown the mountain-side.
Where shall we turn? What issue can there be?
Through the waste woods we searched and found the Tree,
Sole of its kind, bowed with its precious fruit;
And lo, the great snake coiling round the root!
Was all our toil, our patience, then, for this?
Our prayers translated to a brutal hiss?
Our desperate hopes, the fears and dangers passed,
To end in death and terror at the last?
Reach me your hand; the darkness, gathering in,
Shrouds us—for now the mysteries begin:
The world we lost grows dim and yet on high
Figures of courage glitter in the sky;
And, though a desert compasses us around,
Layers of water lie beneath that ground;
The fissure in the rock that sets them free
Feeds and refreshes our Forbidden Tree.
Already, though we do not feel it yet,
The unexpected miracle is complete;
Already, through the midnight hours, unseen
They rise and make these barren places green
Till the parched land in which we lost our way
Gives grace and power and meaning to the day,
Renews the heart, gives joy to every act
And turns the fables into living fact.

If in heroic couplets, then, I seem
To cut the ground from an heroic theme,
It is not that I mock at love, or you,
But, living two lives, know both of them are true.
There's a hard thing, and yet it must be done,
Which is: to see and live them both as one.
The daylight vision is stronger to compel,
But leaves us in the ignorance of hell;
And they, who live by star-light all the time,
Helpless and dangerous, blunder into crime;
And we must learn and live, as yet we may,
Vision that keeps the night and saves the day.

PART TWO

FLOWER POEM

Not these cut heads posed in a breathless room,
Their crisp flesh screaming while the cultured eye
Feeds grublike on the double martyrdom:
The insane virgins lusting as they die!
Connoisseurs breathe the rose's agony;
Between their legs the hairy flowers in bloom

Thrill at the amorous comparison.
As the professor snips the richest bud
For his lapel, his scalpel of reason
Lies on the tray; the class yawns for its food—
Only transfusion of a poem's blood
Can save them, bleeding from their civilization—

Not this cut flower but the entire plant
Achieves its miracle from soil and wind,
Rooted in dung, dirt, dead men's bones; the scent
And glory not in themselves an end; the end:
Fresh seeding in some other dirty mind,
The ache of its mysterious event

As its frail root fractures the subsoil, licks
At the damp stone in passing, drives its life
Deeper to split the ancient bedded rocks
And penetrates the cave beneath, it curls
In horror from that roof. There in its grief
The subterranean river roars, the troll's knife
Winks on his whetstone and the grinning girls
Sit spinning the bright fibre of their sex.

EASTER HYMN

Make no mistake; there will be no forgiveness;
No voice can harm you and no hand will save;
Fenced by the magic of deliberate darkness
You walk on the sharp edges of the wave;

Trouble with soul again the putrefaction
Where Lazarus three days rotten lies content.
Your human tears will be the seed of faction,
Murder the sequel to your sacrament.

The City of God is built like other cities:
Judas negotiates the loans you float;
You will meet Caiaphas upon committees;
You will be glad of Pilate's casting vote.

Your truest lovers still the foolish virgins,
Your heart will sicken at the marriage feasts
Knowing they watch you from the darkened gardens
Being polite to your official guests.

THE WANDERING ISLANDS

You cannot build bridges between the wandering islands;
The Mind has no neighbours, and the unteachable heart
Announces its armistice time after time, but spends
Its love to draw them closer and closer apart.

They are not on the chart; they turn indifferent shoulders
On the island-hunters; they are not afraid
Of Cook or De Quiros, nor of the empire-builders;
By missionary bishops and the tourist trade

They are not annexed; they claim no fixed position;
They take no pride in a favoured latitude;
The committee of atolls inspires in them no devotion
And the earthquake belt no special attitude.

A refuge only for the ship-wrecked sailor;
He sits on the shore and sullenly masturbates,
Dreaming of rescue, the pubs in the ports of call or
The big-hipped harlots at the dock-yard gates.

But the wandering islands drift on their own business,
Incurious whether the whales swim round or under,
Investing no fear in ultimate forgiveness.
If they clap together, it is only casual thunder

And yet they are hurt—for the social polyps never
Girdle their bare shores with a moral reef;
When the icebergs grind them they know both beauty and terror;
They are not exempt from ordinary grief;

And the sudden ravages of love surprise
Them like acts of God—its irresistible function
They have never treated with convenient lies
As a part of geography or an institution.

An instant of fury, a bursting mountain of spray,
They rush together, their promontories lock,
An instant the castaway hails the castaway,
But the sounds perish in that earthquake shock.

And then, in the crash of ruined cliffs, the smother
And swirl of foam, the wandering islands part.
But all that one mind ever knows of another,
Or breaks the long isolation of the heart,

Was in that instant. The shipwrecked sailor senses
His own despair in a retreating face.
Around him he hears in the huge monotonous voices
Of wave and wind: 'The Rescue will not take place.'

ASCENT INTO HELL

Little Henry, too, had a great notion of singing.
HISTORY OF THE FAIRCHILD FAMILY

I, too, at the mid-point, in a well-lit wood
of second-rate purpose and mediocre success,
explore in dreams the never-never of childhood,
groping in daylight for the key of darkness;

revisit, among the morning archipelagoes,
Tasmania, my receding childish island;
unchanged my prehistoric flora grows
within me, marsupial territories extend:

there is the land-locked valley and the river,
the Western Tiers make distance an emotion,
the gum trees roar in the gale, the poplars shiver
at twilight, the church pines imitate an ocean.

There, in the clear night, still I listen, waking
to a crunch of sulky wheels on the distant road;
the marsh of stars reflects a starry croaking;
I hear in the pillow the sobbing of my blood

as the panic of unknown footsteps marching nearer,
till the door opens, the inner world of panic
nightmares that woke me to unawakening terror
birthward resume their still inscrutable traffic.

Memory no more the backward, solid continent,
from island to island of despairing dream
I follow the dwindling soul in its ascent;
the bayonets and the pickelhauben gleam

among the leaves, as, in the poplar tree,
they find him hiding. With an axe he stands
above the German soldiers, hopelessly
chopping the fingers from the climbing hands.

Or, in the well-known house, a secret door
opens on empty rooms from which a stair
leads down to a grey, dusty corridor,
room after room, ominous, still and bare.

He cannot turn back, a lurking horror beckons
round the next corner, beyond each further door.
Sweating with nameless anguish then he wakens;
finds the familiar walls blank as before.

Chased by wild bulls, his legs stick fast with terror.
He reaches the fence at last—the fence falls flat.
Choking, he runs, the trees he climbs will totter
or the cruel horns, like telescopes, shoot out.

At his fourth year the waking life turns inward.
Here on his Easter Island the stone faces
rear meaningless monuments of hate and dread.
Dreamlike within the dream real names and places

survive. His mother comforts him with her body
against the nightmare of the lions and tigers.
Again he is standing in his father's study
lying about his lie, is whipped, and hears

his scream of outrage, valid to this day.
In bed, he fingers his stump of sex, invents
how he took off his clothes and ran away,
slit up his belly with various instruments;

to brood on this was a deep abdominal joy
still recognized as a feeling at the core
of love—and the last genuine memory
is singing 'Jesus Loves Me'—then, no more!

Beyond is a lost country and in vain
I enter that mysterious territory.
Lit by faint hints of memory lies the plain
where from its Null took shape this conscious I

which backward scans the dark—But at my side
the unrecognized Other Voice speaks in my ear,
the voice of my fear, the voice of my unseen guide;
'Who are we, stranger? What are we doing here?'

And through the uncertain gloom, sudden I see
beyond remembered time the imagined entry,
the enormous Birth-gate whispering, '*per me,
per me si va tra la perduta gente.*'

THREE ROMANCES—I

The curtain splits. I face the night
Alone in a great gush of light.
The darkness claps and coughs and cries
And twinkles with its thousand eyes.

The music sobs on the long drawn
Sad prelude of a single horn,
Till, with a crash, it takes the bar
That greets the entrance of the star.

I do not know my cue, the part
Forgotten that I learned by heart,
Only the naked act burns clear
And, in that instant, She is here.

As down the centre of the stage
She stalks in her voluptuous rage,
Light shrieks on her elastic skin,
Her navel widens to a grin.

And, left and right, magnificent,
Her scowling thighs about me bent,
Their fathom of strength and thunder join
To brace the warm spathe of the loin.

The flutes in all this blaze and heat
Their long smooth strokes repeat, repeat,
The violins swiftlier, sweetlier call,
And then the trumpet shatters all.

Down through a hundred raptures I
Slide weakly out of her and lie
Like a wet worm upon the boards,
And nobody at all applauds.

For, as the lights go out, there falls
Starlight among the roofless stalls;
This audience died long ago;
Their bones sit rocking at the show.

The dry weeds shake beside your chair;
Your jaw-bone drops to the parterre;
And, from the lustre, clear and full,
One crystal tinkles on your skull.

Here are the weaving branches
Of that resplendent eye,
The rivers' wandering trenches
Left when the rivers dry.

And through the blank of summer
Their parching channels spread;
The last pools steam and shimmer;
The reeds are brown and dead.

For you are both the season
That brimmed their banks with rain
And the blind, wasting passion
That dries them out again.

The eye, whose large horizons
Were quick with liquid sight,
Now circles in your prison's
Impenetrable light.

THREE ROMANCES—III

How can your eyelids cover
The monsters of your sleep?
Above those pits they hover
And plunge into the deep.

The night of horror falters
About your dreadful dream;
The dead men by their halters
Hang straight; the rivers scream;

Their waters writhe in anguish;
The trees weep helpless tears;
The rusting windmills languish
And groan with windy fears;

And from the hollow mountain
A voice of bestial dread
Wails like a golden fountain
And tells you I am dead.

O, it is true, my darling!
Sleep on and never see
What things come creeping, crawling,
Down here to lie with me.

RAWHEAD AND BLOODY BONES

Rawhead and Bloody Bones
Cuts himself another slice;
Incest, Aquinas owns,
Is a form of avarice.

This Belly too commits,
By a strange and self abuse,
Chin-chopper's tit-bits,
Meat of his own mint, chews.

'Know thyself!' says Tongue's root-
Bulb in the bone sconce:
Belly loves its own fruit,
Sucks on three sins at once.

Soul and Body both do
Thus, until, a limit passed,
Gullet severed, right through
Grisly cud falls at last.

Spare your poet pious groans!
Give the poet no advice!
Rawhead and Bloody Bones,
Cut yourself another slice!

PERSONS FROM PORLOCK

'*On awaking he appeared to himself to have a distinct recollection of the whole, and taking his pen, ink and paper, instantly and eagerly wrote down the lines that are here preserved. At this moment he was unfortunately called out by a person on business from Porlock. . . .*'

PREFATORY NOTE TO *Kubla Khan*

It was unfortunate: Poor S.T.C.!
Once in his life, once only among men,
Once in the process of Eternity,
It happened, and it will not happen again:
His dream unbidden took shape as poetry,
And waking, he recalled it, and his pen
Set down the magic lines—then came the dread
Summons from Porlock and the vision fled.

Fortunate Coleridge! He at least began.
Porlock was tardy, almost missed its cue;
Something at least was saved of *Kubla Khan*,
And Porlock's agent, give the man his due,
Paid him that single visit in the span
Of a long life of three score years and two.
The Ancient Mariner, it is fair to mention,
Escaped the Person's sinister attention.

The Swan of Porlock is a kind of duck;
It quacks and has a large, absurd behind—
Yes, on the whole, the poet was in luck.
Think of his fate had Porlock been less kind;
The paps of Porlock might have given him suck;
Teachers from Porlock organised his mind,
And Porlock's Muse inspired the vapid strain
Of: 'Porlock, Loveliest Village of the Plain!'

71

And had his baffled genius stood the test,
With that one vision which is death to hide
Burning for utterance in the poet's breast,
Porlock might still be trusted to provide
Neighbours from Porlock, culled from Porlock's best,
The sweetest girl in Porlock for his bride,
In due course to surround him with some young
Persons from Porlock, always giving tongue.

Eight hours a day of honest Porlock toil,
And Porlock parties—useless to refuse—
The ritual gardening of Porlock soil,
Would leave him time still for a spare-time Muse—
And when with conscience murdered, wits aboil,
He shook the dust of Porlock from his shoes,
Some would be apt to blame him, some to scoff,
But others kindly come to see him off.

Porlock was gone: the marvellous dream was there.
'In Xanadu . . .'—He knew the words by rote,
Had but to set them down.
                         To his despair
He found a man from Porlock wore his coat,
And thought his thoughts; and, stolid in his chair,
A person fresh from Porlock sat and wrote:
'Amid this tumult Kubla heard from far
Voices of Porlock babbling round the bar.'

THE DINNER

Angels have dined with men, and when they do,
All that they touch and taste takes blessing too.
The world that lies within a night and day,
Ended with evening, all things pass away,
And, a new heaven and a new earth begun,
We meet as two, and touch and smile as one.
Then on my sleeve you lay your brilliant hand
And lead me to the lighted table land.
All things expect you: walls and ceiling swim
In mellower light; the chairs stand straight and trim;
The tables dressed with snow behold you come;
The mouth of every crystal glass is dumb;
The knives and forks in silver order shine
And grace descends upon the food and wine.

Delicate, young and cradled in delight,
You take your seat and bare your teeth to bite—
What is my courage then to suffer this
Miracle of your metamorphosis!
For in that instant I behold the jaws
Of the most terrible of carnivores
Tear at its prey; the ravening human packs
Pull down their terrified victim in its tracks;
The wit, the charm, the grace, the pride of life
Adore the bloody edges of a knife!
The nakedness I had my arms about
Was gorged with death—I see the cayman's snout
Snap the deer's nostrils as they touch the flood;
The tiger's hairy muzzle sweet with blood;
The condor, flapping from the rocky peak,
Light on the carrion, plunge his grisly beak
Into the rotting porridge; through the dark
Slides the lithe, cold torpedo of the shark.
The air, the jungle, the salt, cannibal sea

Hold no more ruthless beast of prey than she.
For her the ox falls snoring in his blood;
The lamb is butchered for her daily food;
Her exquisite mouth, that smiles and tastes the wine,
Has killed by proxy a whole herd of swine—

Her exquisite mouth! As men, when at the worst,
Envy past ills, a vision succeeds the first
For which how gladly would I take again
That vision of the bloody mouths of men!
Now from the ancient past are conjured crude
Terrors of the black cave and the blind wood:
There sits the giant at his monstrous board,
The giantess, massive as her shaggy lord,
Squats at the spit and bastes the sizzling meat,
Dresses the trencher, serves and takes her seat,
And, leaning on the plank her full, warm breasts,
Looks in his face and smiles. He takes and tests
His six-foot knife—the little ribs spring wide;
He cuts the liver steaming from its side.
Talking in deep, soft, grumbling undertones
They gnaw and crack and suck the marrowy bones.
The tit-bits and choice meats they pluck and press
Each on the other, with grave tenderness,
And touch and laugh; their strange, fierce features move
With the delight and confidence of love.
I watch their loves, I see their human feast
With the doomed comprehension of the beast;
I feel the sweat creep through my bristling hair;
Hollow with rage and fear, I crouch and stare,
And hear their great jaws strip and crush and chew,
And know the flesh they rend and tear is you.

TOTENTANZ: THE COQUETTE

Past Midnight! Silent in her charming room,
Nobly proportioned, feminine, richly plain,
One elegant femur balanced across its twin,
Sits her lank guest in the deep armchair's gloom,
The dandy's pose, one hand upon his cane,
A bald skull and a melancholy grin.

Outside a car stops purring at the kerb,
Swift footsteps mount the stair; the door flies wide;
She sweeps in, brilliant as a breaking wave;
The shimmer and swirl of skirts, and the superb
Gesture with which she lays her cloak aside—
The Watcher, sitting silent as the grave,

Thinks of some youthful Antony, in all
The panoply of battle, at the hour
Of victory disarming in the camp.
So in her silks, still sparkling from the ball,
Still breathless in the ecstasy of power,
She balances unseeing, turns up her lamp,

Unpins her torrent of hair, unclasps a jewel,
Moving to music still. The marvellous dress
Slides down; the dazzling gestures gleam and glance
While her tall glass reflects them, as a pool
Mirrors some creature of the wilderness
Rapt in its solitary ritual dance;

Some nubile sorceress at the noon of night,
Flitting by savage tarn or sacred well,
Rapt in the magic invocation of love,
Herself enchanted by that animal rite,
Herself the source and vigour of the spell
That leads an unknown lover to her grove.

75

Now naked to her glass, alive, alone,
In scrutiny or question see her stand
Aware at last of her mysterious guest,
The hollow stare, the rigid mask of bone.
Under her arm the lattice of a hand
Clips cold on the ripe triumph of her breast.

Stiffly she stands, considering awhile
The challenge of the male, the frank embrace.
Then, on one shuddering, voluptuous breath,
Leans back to her gaunt lover with a smile,
Half turning, with her plenitude of grace,
In sensuous surrender to her death.

THE ELEGY

Variations on a theme of the Seventeenth Century

Madam, no more! The time has come to eat.
The spirit of man is nourished, too, with meat.
Those heroes and the warriors of old—
Feasting between their battles made them bold.
When Venus in the west hung out her lamp,
The rattling sons of Mars marched home to camp;
And while around the fires their wounds were dressed,
And tale was matched with tale, and jest with jest,
Flagons of wine and oxen roasted whole
Refreshed their bodies and restored the soul.

Come, leave the bed; put on your dress; efface
Awhile this dazzling armoury of grace!
Flushed and rejoicing from the well-fought fight
Now day lies panting in the arms of night;
The first dews tremble on the darkening field;
Put up your naked weapons, the bright shield
Of triumph glinting to the early stars;
Call our troops home with trumpets from their wars;
And, as wise generals, let them rest and dine
And celebrate our truce with meat and wine.
See, the meek table on our service waits;
The devil in crystal winks beside our plates;
These veterans of love's war we shall repay
And crown with feasts the glories of the day.

Think no disgrace, if now they play a part
Less worthy of the soldiers of the heart.
Though these we led were granted, even as we,
Their moment's draught of immortality,
We do but snatch our instant on the height
And in the valleys still live out the night.

77

Yet they surrender nothing which is theirs.
Nature is frugal in her ministers;
Each to some humbler office must return,
And so must we. Then grudge it not, but learn
In this the noble irony of kind:
These fierce, quick hands that rove and clasp must find
Other employment now with knife and fork;
Our mouths that groaned with joy, now eat and talk;
These chief commanders, too, without debate,
Sink to the lowliest service of the state.
Only our eyes observe no armistice;
Sparkling with love's perpetual surprise,
Their bright vedettes keep watch from hill to hill
And, when they meet, renew the combat still.
And yet to view you would I linger on:
This is the rarest moment, soonest gone.
While now the marching stars invest the sky
And the wide lands beneath surrendered lie,
Their streams and forests, parks and fields and farms,
Like this rich empire tranquil in my arms,
Seem lovelier in the last withdrawing light
And, as they vanish, most enchant the sight.
Still let me watch those countries as they fade
And all their lucid contours sink in shade;
The mounting thighs, the line of flank and breast,
Yet harbour a clear splendour from the west;
Though twilight draws into its shadowy reign
This breathing valley and that glimmering plain,
Still let my warrior heart with fresh delight
Rove and reflect: 'Here, here began the fight;
Between those gentle hills I paused to rest,
And on this vale the kiss of triumph pressed;
There, full encircled by the frantic foe,
I rode between the lilies and the snow;
And, in this copse that parts the dark and shine,
Plundered the treasures of the hidden mine;
Down those long slopes in slow retreat I drew;

And here renewed the charge; and here, anew
Met stroke with stroke and touched, at the last breath,
The unimagined ecstasy of death.'

Full darkness! Time enough the lamps were lit.
Let us to dinner, Madam; wine and wit
Must have their hour, even as love and war,
And what's to come revives what went before.
Come now, for see the Captain of my lust,
He that so stoutly fought and stiffly thrust,
Fallen, diminished on the field he lies;
Cover his face, he dreams in paradise.
We, while he sleeps, shall dine; and, when that's done,
Drink to his resurrection later on.

LAMBKIN: A FABLE

A Lamb, that had gone much astray,
Among the mountains lost his way,
His heart, his fleece, alike were black;
He staggered on the stony track;
Grim cliffs and crags above him towered;
Below the precipices loured;
The eagles watching from the height
Observed: 'He will be ours by night';
And, as he reached the line of snow,
Night gathered in the vale below.
The cold was fierce, the barren pass
Scarce offered him one blade of grass.
Alone, unshepherded, his state
Was little less than desperate,
As down he laid his aching bones
Among the hard, unmothering stones,
And on that bleak and bitter air
Bleated a chance, belated prayer.

What was his joy—he lay in doubt—
His bleat was answered by a shout!
Feebly he rose and answered back:
A cheerful hail rang up the track,
And soon, quite safe from hurts and harms,
He lay in the Good Shepherd's arms.

Through the long hours of dark, as they
Towards the fold retraced their way,
He wept indeed, but not for shame
To view the wicked way he came,
Nor fear to meet the master's wrath
Threatened upon his setting forth,
Nor keen repentance at his fall,
But joy to be alive at all.

And yet his tears, as is the case
When the heart turns and cries for grace,
Availed him more than he could know
And washed his black soul white as snow.
At length the weary way was done
Just at the rising of the sun,
And, issuing from a bleak defile,
They saw the dewy pastures smile,
The sheep-cotes and the homely fold,
The crested mountains touched with gold.
And, when he was set down at last,
A sudden tremor through him passed,
For lo, his fleece, once black as night,
Was now a pure and dazzling white!

Who now so glad as Lambkin? Who
Resolved to make his life anew?
The same dull round from day to day
He trod and found it fresh and gay;
No task too hard, no toil too long:
'My pains are given to make me strong.'
Such inward, burning joy to feel
Made him the paragon of zeal;
And then the Shepherd, always near,
Would fondle him and smile to hear
His children pat and pet and praise
The Lamb who learned to mend his ways.
So Lambkin felt as good as gold.
Alas, he found within the fold,
Among his fellow tups and ewes,
Less disposition to enthuse;
For when they greeted him their eyes
Showed neither scandal nor surprise;
They did not seem impressed to learn
His perils or his safe return,
And some were even heard to say:
'Why, Lambkin, have you been away?'

His deadly sins, this new-won grace
That made his such a special case
Alike ignored, he felt his fall
Had scarcely been remarked at all.

No matter! Fire-new virtue asks
Increasing tests and heavier tasks;
The soul unproved can still invent
Worse trials than those by Heaven sent
And finds, of all, the hardest part
To humble the too-eager heart.
So Lambkin found. Though not content,
He bore his modest punishment,
Yet still contrived with Heaven's decrees
To dot the i's and cross the t's.
First at the Shepherd's call and first
Afield, he always chose the worst
And rankest pasture; at the pool
Drank last his muddy belly-full.
When other lambs were at their pranks,
He cropped beside his parents' flanks;
Spied the wolf's ears behind the rock
And was the first to warn the flock;
On dog-days chose the scantiest shade;
Faced drench and tailing unafraid
And for the shearing nursed his wool:
'Lord, help me make it Three Bags Full!'

Alas for virtue and for zeal!
As summer passed, he came to feel,
Compared with him, his fellow sheep
Too much inclined to sloth and sleep.
The Nine and Ninety, faithful crew,
Though they were guiltless, it was true,
Had never strayed, would not rebel,
Were somewhat slack in doing well.
Afold the wethers would complain

Of wind and dust, or mud and rain;
Afield the ewes would criticise
The sheep-dog's temper, or the flies;
The rams were prone, in good or bad,
To take for granted what they had;
And all complained with ill-concealed
Annoyance, when he led the field:
'Go easy; do you have to trot?
Lambkin, you make the pace too hot!'

'My friends,' he answered them at last,
'The time for diffidence is past.
The crimes for which I now atone,
My shame and guilt, I freely own;
And I, the least among you here,
Would hold my peace, did I not fear
That even while I hesitate
To warn you, it may be too late.
Unworthy as I am and weak,
Hear, then, what conscience bids me speak:

'My tale, as most of you should know,
Begins one day six months ago
When, black without and foul within,
Leprous and ulcerate with sin,
The Shepherd snatched me, ere I fell,
Back from the very brink of Hell.
O for a tongue that could express
That moment of pure happiness!
Once more within the fold I stood,
Renewed by Grace, redeemed by Blood.
At first with tears I viewed the place
And every dear, familiar face;
It seemed, through dim and weeping eyes,
A little short of Paradise.

But soon, forgive if I speak plain,
My tears were dry; I looked again.
This fold, which seemed at first so fair,
Had an ill-kept, neglected air;
The troughs were split, the stalls awry,
Through crazy timbers showed the sky;
Sheep-tods and puddles on the floor
And tailings mixed with shabby straw;
The lambs unruly, and the ewes
Gossips too apt to air their views;
The wethers envious of the tups;
The rams vainglorious in their cups;
The watch-dog slack; the sheep-dog sly;
Bedraggled wool and udders dry—
Such was the picture; and—I blame
My silence—it is still the same.

'You do not see it thus, 'tis true;
You could not be expected to.
Habit is strong and makes us blind.
Indeed, though it may seem unkind
To mention this, there have been times
When I have almost blessed the crimes
Which, deadly as they are, may be
A means of Grace to make us see.

'There have been times when I have stood
Chewing my conscientious cud,
Erect, to save this spotless fleece,
While in the dust you took your ease
Careless of dirt and keds and burrs,
When I have wondered: was it worse
To stay at home or to rebel?
Or was I even—who can tell?—
Upon that dark and fatal day
Led providentially astray?

'We are but sheep, and as we can
Must strive to guess the Shepherd's plan;
And yet, what other can it be
Than this: to touch your hearts through *me*?
Look, then, on me and rise and shine
And win a fleece as white as mine!'

The words were scarcely out before
First smiles, then sniggers, then a roar
Of helpless laughter shook the fold.
Again it rose; again it rolled,
While Lambkin, taken by surprise,
Stared back with grieved and puzzled eyes;
And next chagrin, and last dismay
Possessed him, and he ran away.

Away! Still followed by their rude,
Hilarious ingratitude,
He passed the mustering pens, the race,
The shearing shed, and none gave chase.
No voice behind cried: 'Lambkin, wait!'
He reached the open pasture gate
And passed the empty fields, and took
A sheep-pad leading to the brook;
And, stooping to the pool, he saw
What all the merriment was for:
The face reflected in the pool
Was his, and his for sure the wool,
Except that all he viewed below
Showed black as pitch from top to toe.

MAN FRIDAY

For John Pringle

Saved at long last through Him whose power to save
Kept from the walking, as the watery grave,
Crusoe returned to England and his kind,
Proof that an unimaginative mind
And sober industry and commonsense
May supplement the work of Providence.
He, no less providential, and no less
Inscrutably resolved to save and bless,
Eager to share his fortune with the weak
And faithful servants whom he taught to speak,
By all his years of exile undeterred,
Took into exile Friday and the bird.

The bird no doubt was well enough content.
She had her corn—what matter where she went?
Except when once a week he walked to church,
She had her master's shoulder as a perch,
She shared the notice of the crowds he drew
Who praised her language and her plumage too,
And like a rational female could be gay
On admiration and three meals a day.

But Friday, the dark Caribbean man,
Picture his situation if you can:
The gentle savage, taught to speak and pray,
On England's Desert Island cast away,
No godlike Crusoe issuing from his cave
Comes with his thunderstick to slay and save;
Instead from caves of stone, as thick as trees,
More dreadful than ten thousand savages,
In their strange clothes and monstrous mats of hair,
The pale-eyed English swarm to joke and stare,
With endless questions round him crowd and press
Curious to see and touch his loneliness.

Unlike his master Crusoe long before
Crawling half-drowned upon the desolate shore,
Mere ingenuity useless in his need,
No wreck supplies him biscuit, nails and seed,
No fort to build, no call to bake, to brew,
Make pots and pipkins, cobble coat and shoe,
Gather his rice and milk his goats, and rise
Daily to some absorbing enterprise.

And yet no less than Crusoe he must find
Some shelter for the solitary mind;
Some daily occupation too contrive
To warm his wits and keep the heart alive;
Protect among the cultured, if he can,
The 'noble savage' and the 'natural man'.
As Crusoe made his clothes, so he no less
Must labour to invent his nakedness
And, lest their alien customs without trace
Absorb him, tell the legends of his race
Each night aloud in the soft native tongue,
That filled his world when, bare and brown and young,
His brown, bare mother held him at her breast,
Then say his English prayers and sink to rest.
And each day waking in his English sheets,
Hearing the waggons in the cobbled streets,
The morning bells, the clatter and cries of trade,
He must recall, within their palisade,
The sleeping cabins in the tropic dawn,
The rapt, leaf-breathing silence, and the yawn
Of naked children as they wake and drowse,
The women chattering round their fires, the prows
Of wet canoes nosing the still lagoon;
At each meal, handling alien fork or spoon,
Remember the spiced mess of yam and fish
And the brown fingers meeting in the dish;
Remember too those island feasts, the sweet
Blood frenzy and the taste of human meat.

Thus he piled memories against his need:
In vain! For still he found the past recede.
Try as he would, recall, relive, rehearse,
The cloudy images would still disperse,
Till, as in dreams, the island world he knew
Confounded the fantastic with the true,
While England, less unreal day by day,
The Cannibal Island, ate his past away.
But for the brooding eye, the swarthy skin,
That witnessed to the Natural Man within,
Year following year, by inches, as they ran,
Transformed the savage to an Englishman.
Brushed, barbered, hatted, trousered and baptized,
He looked, if not completely civilized,
What came increasingly to be the case:
An upper servant, conscious of his place,
Friendly but not familiar in address
And prompt to please, without obsequiousness,
Adept to dress, to shave, to carve, to pour
And skilled to open or refuse the door,
To keep on terms with housekeeper and cook,
But quell the maids and footmen with a look.
And now his master, thoughtful for his need,
Bought him a wife and gave him leave to breed.
A fine mulatto, once a lady's maid,
She thought herself superior to Trade
And, reared on a Plantation, much too good
For a low native Indian from the wood;
Yet they contrived at last to rub along
For he was strong and kind, and she was young,
And soon a father, then a family man,
Friday took root in England and began
To be well thought of in the little town,
And quoted in discussions at 'The Crown',
Whether the Funds would fall, the French would treat
Or the new ministry could hold its seat.
For though he seldom spoke, the rumour ran

88

The master had no secrets from his man,
And Crusoe's ventures prospered so, in short,
It was concluded he had friends at Court.

Yet as the years of exile came and went,
Though first he grew resigned and then content,
Had you observed him close, you might surprise
A stranger looking through the servant's eyes.
Some colouring of speech, some glint of pride,
Not born of hope, for hope long since had died,
Not even desire, scarce memory at last,
Preserved that stubborn vestige of the past.

It happened once that man and master made
A trip together on affairs of trade;
A ship reported foundered in the Downs
Brought them to visit several seaport towns.
At one of these, Great Yarmouth or King's Lynn,
Their business done, they baited at an inn,
And in the night were haunted by the roar
Of a wild wind and tide against the shore.
Crusoe soon slept again, but Friday lay
Awake and listening till the dawn of day.
For the first time in all his exiled years
The thunder of the ocean filled his ears;
And that tremendous voice so long unheard
Released and filled and drew him, till he stirred
And left the house and passed the town, to reach
At last the dunes and rocks and open beach:
Pale, bare and gleaming in the break of day
A sweep of new-washed sand around the bay,
And spindrift driving up the bluffs like smoke,
As the long combers reared their crests and broke.
There in the sand beside him Friday saw
A single naked footprint on the shore.

His heart stood still, for as he stared, he knew
The foot that made it never had worn shoe
And, at a glance, that no such walker could
Have been a man of European blood.
From such a footprint once he could describe
If not the owner's name, at least his tribe,
And tell his purpose as men read a face
And still his skill sufficed to know the race;
For this was such a print as long ago
He too had made and taught his eyes to know.
There could be no mistake. Awhile he stood
Staring at that grey German Ocean's flood;
And suddenly he saw those shores again
Where Orinoco pours into the main,
And, stunned with an incredible surmise,
Heard in his native tongue once more the cries
Of spirits silent now for many a day;
And all his years of exile fell away.

The sun was nearly to the height before
Crusoe arrived hallooing at the shore,
Followed the footprints to the beach and found
The clothes and shoes and thought his servant drowned.
Much grieved he sought him up and down the bay
But never guessed, when later in the day
They found the body drifting in the foam,
That Friday had been rescued and gone home.

A BIDDING GRACE

For what we are about to hear, Lord, Lord,
The dreadful judgement, the unguessed reprieve,
The brief, the battering, the jubilant chord
Of trumpets quickening this guilty dust,
Which still would hide from what it shall receive,
Lord, make us thankful to be what we must.

For what we are now about to lose, reprove,
Assuage or comfort, Lord, this greedy flesh,
Still grieving, still rebellious, still in love,
Still prodigal of treasure still unspent.
Teach the blood weaving through its intricate mesh
The sigh, the solace, the silence of consent.

For what we are about to learn too late, too late
To save, though we repent with tears of blood:
The innocent ruined, the gentle taught to hate,
The love we made a means to its despair—
For all we have done or did not when we could,
Redouble on us the evil these must bear.

For what we are about to say, urge, plead,
The specious argument, the lame excuse,
Prompt our contempt. When these archangels read
Our trivial balance, lest the shabby bill
Tempt to that abjectness which begs or sues,
Leave us one noble impulse: to be still.

For what we are about to act, the lust, the lie
That works unbidden, even now restrain
This reckless heart. Though doomed indeed to die,
Grant that we may, still trembling at the bar
Of Justice in the thud of fiery rain,
Acknowledge at last the truth of what we are.

In all we are about to receive, last, last,
Lord, help us bear our part with all men born
And, after judgement given and sentence passed,
Even at this uttermost, measured in thy gaze,
Though in thy mercy, for the rest to mourn,
Though in thy wrath we stand, to stand and praise.

THE DAMNATION OF BYRON

When the great hero, adding to the charms
of genius and his scandals, left the light
stamped with the irresistible trade of arms,
the Hell of Women received him as their right.

Through the Infernal Fields he makes his way
playing again, but on a giant stage,
his own Don Juan; pursuing day by day
Childe Harold's last astonishing pilgrimage.

It is the landscape of erotic dreams:
the dim, brown plains, the country without air
or tenderness of trees by hidden streams,
but cactus or euphorbia here and there

thrusts up its monstrous phallus at the sky.
And moving against this silvered, lustrous green
like a pink larva over the whole dry
savannah of hell, the bodies of women are seen.

And at his coming all their beauties stir
mysterious, like the freshening of a rose
as, the incomparable connoisseur,
pale and serene across their world he goes,

always there rises glowing in his path,
superb and sensual, in the light that pours
a tarnished glory on the soil of death,
this leafless nakedness of tropic flowers;

the female body's impersonal charm, the curves
of a young head poised on its gracious stalk.
The idiom of her gesture he observes,
that tender dislocation of her walk.

Held in his brain's deep lupanar they float,
the tapering trunk, the pure vase of the hips,
the breasts, the breasts to which the hands go out
instinctive, the adoring finger-tips,

the thighs incurved, the skin misted with light,
the mouth repeating its own rich circumflex . . .
At first he moves and breathes in his delight
drowned in the brute somnambulism of sex.

He is a kind of symbol of the male:
as a great bull, stiffly, deliberately
crosses his paddock, lashing his brutal tail,
the sullen engine of fecundity,

so, in his first youth and his first desire,
his air of pride and the immortal bloom,
once more he sets the feminine world on fire,
passing in his romantic blaze of gloom.

Prodigious vigour flowers new in him:
each morning nerves him with heroic lust.
His thoughts are women, he breathes, is clothed with them,
he sinks on something female in the dust.

He has them all, all the menagerie
of race, the subtle stimulus of shapes:
Negresses in their first nubility
with the sad eyes and muzzles of young apes,

vast Scandinavian divinities
superbly modelled, for all their cowlike air,
the pale bread of their bellies magnificent rise
from the blond triangle of pubic hair,

94

and slender girls with delicate golden shanks
and elongated skulls from lost Peru . . .
and sensual emphasis of the Spaniard's flanks,
and the callipygous haunches of the Jew. . . .

Dancers and whores, blue-stockings, countesses,
types of La Fornarina and Caroline Lamb,
all the seductions of all mistresses,
the savage, the sentimental and the sham . . .

And yet he is alone. At first he feels
nothing above the tumult of his blood,
while through his veins like the slow pox there steals
the deep significance of his solitude.

And from this feeling without haste or pause
vengeance predestined sharpens, bit by bit;
as lust its anaesthesia withdraws
the force of his damnation grows from it.

Grows as the mind wakes, and inexorably
the critic, the thinker, the invincible
intelligence at last detached and free
wakes, and he knows . . . he knows he is in hell.

And there begins in him that horrible thing,
clairvoyance, the cruel nightmare of escape:
He seeks companions: but they only bring
wet kisses and voluptuous legs agape . . .

He longs for the companionship of men,
their sexless friendliness. He cannot live
'like the gods in Lucretius once again'
nor ever in woman's wit and charm forgive

the taint of the pervading feminine.
Yet always to this nausea he returns
from his own mind—the emptiness within
of the professional lover. As he learns

how even his own society has become
a horror, a loneliness he cannot bear,
the last stage of Don Juan's martyrdom,
the last supreme resources of despair

appear, and brutally lucid he descends
simply to treat them as The Enemy.
His lust becomes revenge, his ardour lends
insatiable pleasure to his insanity.

As he exhausts himself in the delights
of torture, gourmandising in their pain,
hate eats his features out: it seethes and bites
like a slow acid. It destroys his brain.

Yet this resource betrays him, even this,
for like tormented demons, they adore
their torment. They revere like savages
the god's ferocity with lascivious awe.

Until, neurotic, hounded by strange fears,
at last his journey changes to a flight.
Delirious, broken, fugitive, he hears
marching and countermarching in the night,

the panic of vague terrors closing in:
whichever way he turns he hears them come.
Far off immeasurable steps begin,
far off the ominous mumble of a drum,

and from the bounds of that dim listening land
approaches with her grave incessant tread
the Eternal Goddess in whose placid hand
are all the happy and all the rebellious dead.

Before her now he stands and makes his prayer
for that oblivion of the Second Death . . .
when suddenly those majestic breasts all bare
riding the tranquil motion of her breath

reveal the body of her divinity:
the torso spread marmoreal, his eyes
downwards uncover its mighty line and see
darkness dividing those prodigious thighs.

There as he stares, slowly she smiles at him . . .
And the great hero, mad with the terrible
madness of souls, turns fleeing, while the dim
plains heave with the immense derision of Hell.

THE KINGS

The lion in deserts royally takes his prey;
Gaunt crags cast back the hunting eagle's scream.
The King of Parasites, delicate, white and blind,
Ruling his world of fable even as they,
Dreams out his greedy and imperious dream
Immortal in the bellies of mankind.

In a rich bath of pre-digested soup,
Warm in the pulsing bowel, safely shut
From the bright ambient horror of sun and air,
His slender segments ripening loop by loop,
Broods the voluptuous monarch of the gut,
The Tapeworm, the prodigious Solitaire.

Alone among the royal beasts of prey
He takes no partner, no imperial mate
Seeks his embrace and bears his clamorous brood;
Within himself, in soft and passionate play,
Two sexes in their vigour celebrate
The raptures of helminthine solitude.

From the barbed crown that hooks him to his host,
The limbless ribbon, fecund, flat and wet,
Sways as the stream's delicious juices move;
And, as the ripe joints rupture and are lost,
Quivers in the prolonged, delirious jet
And spasm of unremitting acts of love.

And Nature no less prodigal in birth
In savage profusion spreads his royal sway:
Herds are his nurseries till the mouths of men,
At public feasts, or the domestic hearth,
Or by the hands of children at their play,
Transmit his line to human flesh again.

The former times, as emblems of an age,
Graved the gier-eagle's pride, the lion's great heart,
Leviathan sporting in the perilous sea;
Pictured on History's or the Muse's page,
All knew the King, the Hero, set apart
To stand up stiff against calamity,

Breed courage amid a broken nation's groans,
Cherish the will in men about to die,
To chasten with just rule a barbarous tribe
And guard, at last, the earth that kept his bones.
And still the Muse, who does not flatter or lie,
Finds for our age a symbol to describe

The secret life of Technocratic Man,
Abject desire, base fear that shape his law,
His idols of the cave, the mart, the stye—
No lion at bay for a beleaguered clan,
No eagle with the serpent in his claw,
Nor dragon soter with his searing eye,

But the great, greedy, parasitic worm,
Sucking the life of nations from within,
Blind and degenerate, snug in excrement.
'Behold your dream!' she says, 'View here the form
And mirror of Time, the Shape you trusted in
While your world crumbled and my heavens were rent.'

AUSTRALIA

A Nation of trees, drab green and desolate grey
In the field uniform of modern wars,
Darkens her hills, those endless, outstretched paws
Of Sphinx demolished or stone lion worn away.

They call her a young country, but they lie:
She is the last of lands, the emptiest,
A woman beyond her change of life, a breast
Still tender but within the womb is dry.

Without songs, architecture, history:
The emotions and superstitions of younger lands,
Her rivers of water drown among inland sands,
The river of her immense stupidity

Floods her monotonous tribes from Cairns to Perth.
In them at last the ultimate men arrive
Whose boast is not: 'we live' but 'we survive',
A type who will inhabit the dying earth.

And her five cities, like five teeming sores,
Each drains her: a vast parasite robber-state
Where second-hand Europeans pullulate
Timidly on the edge of alien shores.

Yet there are some like me turn gladly home
From the lush jungle of modern thought, to find
The Arabian desert of the human mind,
Hoping, if still from the deserts the prophets come,

Such savage and scarlet as no green hills dare
Springs in that waste, some spirit which escapes
The learned doubt, the chatter of cultured apes
Which is called civilization over there.

PART THREE

A COMMINATION

Like John on Patmos, brooding on the Four
Last Things, I meditate the ruin of friends
Whose loss, Lord, brings this grand new Curse to mind.
Now send me foes worth cursing, or send more
—Since means should be proportionate to ends—
For mine are few and of the piddling kind:

Drivellers, snivellers, writers of bad verse,
Backbiting bitches, snipers from a pew,
Small turds from the great arse of self-esteem;
On such as these I would not waste my curse.
God send me soon the enemy or two
Fit for the wrath of God, of whom I dream:

Some Caliban of Culture, some absurd
Messiah of the Paranoiac State,
Some Educator wallowing in his slime,
Some Prophet of the Uncreating Word
Monsters and man might reasonably hate,
Masters of Progress, Leaders of our Time;

But chiefly the Suborners: Common Tout
And Punk, the Advertiser, him I mean
And his smooth hatchet-man, the Technocrat,
Them let my malediction single out,
These modern Dives with their talking screen
Who lick the sores of Lazarus and grow fat,

Licensed to pimp, solicit and procure
Here in my house, to foul my feast, to bawl
Their wares while I am talking with my friend,
To pour into my ears a public sewer
Of all the Strumpet Muses sell and all
That prostituted science has to vend.

In this great Sodom of a world, which turns
The Treasure of the Intellect to dust
And every gift to some perverted use,
What wonder if the human spirit learns
Recourses of despair or of disgust,
Abortion, suicide and self-abuse.

But let me laugh, Lord; let me crack and strain
The belly of this derision till it burst;
For I have seen too much, have lived too long
A citizen of Sodom to refrain,
And in the stye of Science, from the first,
Have watched the pearls of Circe drop on dung.

Let me not curse my children, nor in rage
Mock at the just, the helpless and the poor,
Foot-fast in Sodom's rat-trap; make me bold
To turn on the Despoilers all their age
Invents: damnations never felt before
And hells more horrible than hot and cold.

And, since in Heaven creatures purified,
Rational, free, perfected in their kinds
Contemplate God and see Him face to face,
In Hell, for sure, spirits transmogrified,
Paralysed wills and parasitic minds
Mirror their own corruption and disgrace.

Now let this curse fall on my enemies,
My enemies, Lord, but all mankind's as well,
Prophets and panders of their golden calf;
Let Justice fit them all in their degrees;
Let them, still living, know that state of hell,
And let me see them perish, Lord, and laugh.

Let them be glued to television screens
Till their minds fester and the trash they see
Worm their dry hearts away to crackling shells;
Let ends be so revenged upon their means
That all that once was human grows to be
A flaccid mass of phototropic cells;

Let the dog love his vomit still, the swine
Squelch in the slough; and let their only speech
Be Babel; let the specious lies they bred
Taste on their tongues like intellectual wine;
Let sung commercials surfeit them, till each
Goggles with nausea in his nauseous bed.

And, lest with them I learn to gibber and gloat,
Lead me, for Sodom is my city still,
To seek those hills in which the heart finds ease;
Give Lot his leave; let Noah build his boat,
And me and mine, when each has laughed his fill,
View thy damnation and depart in peace.

STANDARDISATION

When, darkly brooding on this Modern Age,
the journalist with his marketable woes
fills up once more the inevitable page
of fatuous, flatulent, Sunday-paper prose;

whenever the green aesthete starts to whoop
with horror at the house not made with hands
and when from vacuum cleaners and tinned soup
another pure theosophist demands

rebirth in other, less industrial stars
where huge towns thrust up in synthetic stone
and films and sleek miraculous motor cars
and celluloid and rubber are unknown;

when from his vegetable Sunday School
emerges with the neatly maudlin phrase
still one more Nature poet, to rant or drool
about the 'Standardisation of the Race';

I see, stooping among her orchard trees,
the old, sound Earth, gathering her windfalls in,
broad in the hams and stiffening at the knees,
pause, and I see her grave malicious grin.

For there is no manufacturer competes
with her in the mass production of shapes and things.
Over and over she gathers and repeats
the cast of a face, a million butterfly wings.

She does not tire of the pattern of a rose.
Her oldest tricks still catch us with surprise.
She cannot recall how long ago she chose
the streamlined hulls of fish, the snail's long eyes,

Love, which still pours into its ancient mould
the lashing seed that grows to a man again,
from whom by the same processes unfold
unending generations of living men.

She has standardised his ultimate needs and pains.
Lost tribes in a lost language mutter in
his dreams: his science is tethered to their brains,
his guilt merely repeats Original Sin.

And beauty standing motionless before
her mirror sees behind her, mile on mile,
a long queue in an unknown corridor,
anonymous faces plastered with her smile.

THE AGE OF INNOCENCE

or DARWIN MORALIZED

*'. . . and therefore you must not grudge to find the same soul in an
Emperor, in a Post-horse, and in a Mushroom, since no unreadiness in the
soul, but an indisposition in the organs works this. And therefore though
this soul could not move when it was a Melon, yet it may remember and
now tell me, at what lascivious banquet it was served. And though it
could not speak when it was a spider, yet it can remember, and now tell
me, who used it for poison to attain dignity.'*

JOHN DONNE

'That was the Eocene, the Golden Age;
On the vast plains of that lost continent'
—the Lecturer coughed and paused to turn a page—
'Swarmed the first men, hairy and innocent,
And browsed and bred and slept and were content,
Their only speech short cries of joy and rage.

'Observe this skull: they were, as you can see,
Small-brained and simple hearted, largely thewed.
Recent research in archæology
Has proved the males magnificently endued
With virile force, the females handsome, nude,
Generous and quite devoid of coquetry.

'A touch, a nod, and Nature did the rest:
Their loins were fruitful and the world was wide.
If I may be allowed a simple jest,
They could not count, but how they multiplied!
The earth with prodigal hand their wants supplied;
We might suppose them, then, supremely blest.

108

'Alas, we would be wrong: the state of man
Has never known uncomplicated bliss.
Like other species since the world began,
Natural selection makes him what he is.
The great Darwinian hypothesis
Knows no exception to its general plan.

'Nature provides a process of control
On her own limitless fecundity;
Each kind evolves to its mysterious goal
Thanks to some ruthless natural enemy.
The fittest to survive, survive. We see
In this the explanation of the soul.

'In these primordial men, I should explain,
Two types of primitive soul distinguished two
Species, and each a pure Mendelian strain;
The evidence suggests that each bred true.
One type was white and dazzling to the view;
One a soft black—' the Lecturer paused again,

Took off his spectacles and gazed around,
Then, delicately polishing each glass,
Replaced them magisterially and frowned.
'The soul of modern man,' he told the class,
'Occurs in various shades of *grey*. Alas,
The old pure strains today are rarely found.

'But let us contemplate the Eocene
As it would be if we could travel back:
Men in unnumbered millions rove the green
And flowery lap of earth. Some have the knack
To hunt and snare small prey: their souls are black.
(Doubtless, some melanism in the gene.)

'They showed more wit than the albino kind,
Whose habits, strictly vegetarian,
Prove them more brutish, while the blacks inclined
More to the brutal: but at best we can
Hardly allow them, placed by modern man,
More than a rudimentary sort of mind.

'Over the heads of this dumb, wandering horde,
Darkening the sky, filling the reach of space,
Clouds of voracious spirits wheeled and soared,
Following their natural prey, the human race:
Angels, descending with rich cries of grace,
Exulted in the bounty of the Lord;

'While swarms of demons flocking to the spot,
Swooped down, with hideous shrieks of rage and hate,
To seize and rend their victims as they squat
At meat, or tear them while they copulate.
Yet, delicate feeders these, no flesh they ate,
Sucked the sweet souls and left the rest to rot.

'That crude black taste, the demons' chief delight,
Is something that the angels all detest;
While the bland milky flavours of the white
Sicken a healthy demon at the best.
But none for the rare *greys* showed any zest,
Fruit of mischance or blunders of the night.

'It follows, gentlemen, you will observe'
—the Lecturer beamed around the class and winked—
'That, following an asymptotic curve,
Both the pure species soon became extinct.
The Chain of Cause, inexorably linked,
Laid bare by that great science which we serve,

'Thus demonstrates the Progress of the Soul.
Throwbacks to black or white, indeed, arise;
But Nature in ourselves attains her goal:
The triumph of Adaptive Compromise!
In the grey eye of Science alone it lies
To see life steadily and see it whole.'

THE HOUSE OF GOD

Morning service! parson preaches;
People all confess their sins;
God's domesticated creatures
Twine and rub against his shins;

Tails erect and whiskers pricking,
Sleeking down their Sunday fur,
Though demure, alive and kicking,
All in unison they purr:

'Lord we praise Thee; hear us Master!
Feed and comfort, stroke and bless!
And not too severely cast a
Glance upon our trespasses:

'Yesterday we were not able
To resist that piece of fish
Left upon the kitchen table
While You went to fetch the dish;

'Twice this week a scrap with Rover;
Once, at least, we missed a rat;
And we *do* regret, Jehovah,
Having kittens in Your hat!

'Sexual noises in the garden,
Smelly patches in the hall—
Hear us, Lord, absolve and pardon;
We are human after all!'

Home at last from work in Heaven,
This is all the rest God gets;
Gladly for one day in seven
He relaxes with His pets.

Looking down He smiles and ponders,
Thinks of something extra nice:
From His beard, O Joy, O wonders!
Falls a shower of little mice.

THE BRIDES

Down the assembly line they roll and pass
Complete at last, a miracle of design;
Their chromium fenders, the unbreakable glass,
The fashionable curve, the air-flow line.

Grease to the elbows Mum and Dad enthuse,
Pocket their spanners and survey the bride;
Murmur: 'A sweet job! All she needs is juice!
Built for a life-time—sleek as a fish. Inside

'He will find every comfort: the full set
Of gadgets; knobs that answer to the touch
For light or music; a place for his cigarette;
Room for his knees; a honey of a clutch.'

Now slowly through the show-room's flattering glare
See her wheeled in to love, console, obey,
Shining and silent! Parson with a prayer
Blesses the number-plate, she rolls away

To write her numerals in his book of life;
And now, at last, stands on the open road,
Triumphant, perfect, every inch a wife,
While the corks pop, the flash-light bulbs explode.

Her heavenly bowser-boy assumes his seat;
She prints the soft dust with her brand-new treads,
Swings towards the future, purring with a sweet
Concatenation of the poppet heads.

THE RETURN FROM THE FREUDIAN ISLANDS

When they heard Sigmund the Saviour in these coasts
the islanders were very much impressed;
abandoned the worship of their fathers' ghosts
and dedicated temples to their guest,

shocked and delighted as the saint revealed
the unacknowledged body and made them see,
suppressed by corsets, morbidly concealed
in cotton combinations, neck to knee,

how it bred night-sweats, the disease of shame,
corns, fluxions, baldness and the sense of sin,
how clothes to the Analytic Eye became
fantasies, furtive symbols of the skin.

At first the doctrine took them all by storm;
urged to be stark, they peeled as they were told;
forgetting their rags had also kept them warm,
for the island climate is often extremely cold.

And if the old, the wry, the ugly shared
some natural reluctance to begin it,
enthusiasts all, the young at once declared
their Brave Nude world, that had such people in it.

Till some discovered that stripping to the buff
only exposed the symbol of The Hide:
its sinister pun unmasked, it must come off,
the saint must preach The Visible Inside!

The saint, though somewhat startled at this view,
trapped by the logic of his gospel, spent
some time in prayer, and in a week or two,
to demonstrate the new experiment,

breastless and bald, with ribbed arms, lashless eyes,
in intricate bandages of human meat,
with delicate ripple and bulge of muscled thighs,
the first skinned girl walked primly down the street.

Though there were many to admire her charms:
the strappings and flexures of twig-like toes, the skeins
and twisted sensitive cables of her arms,
the pectoral fans, the netting of nerves and veins:

yet those who followed her example found
one lack—till Sigmund undertook to prove
how much their late behaviour centred round
a common skin disease they had called love.

And for a time they thoroughly enjoyed
the brisk intolerance of the purified,
in sects and schisms before The Holy Freud
self-torn—while lesser saints were deified.

Till Faith, which never can let well alone,
from heresy and counter-heresy
prompted the saint to bare beneath the bone
The Ultimate Visceral Reality.

Long time he mused before The Sacred Id,
long prayed, before he finally began
and, purged, impersonal, uninhibited,
produced at last The Basic Freudian Man.

At the Fertility Festival that year
the skinned men blushed to see the skeleton,
a bone-cage filled with female guts appear
tottering before them in the midday sun.

Its slats and levering rods they saw, the full
cogged horseshoe grin of two and thirty teeth,
the frantic eyeballs swivelling in the skull,
the swagging human umbles underneath,

the soft wet mottled granite of the lung
bulge and collapse, the liver worn askew
jauntily quiver, the plump intestines hung
in glistening loops and bolsters in their view,

and clear through gut and bowel the mashy chyme
churn downward; jelled in its transparent sheath
the scowling foetus tethered, and the time-
bomb tumour set unguessed its budded death.

And while for them with mannequin grace she swayed
her pelvis, Sigmund, so that none should miss
the beauty of the new world he had made,
explained The Triumph of Analysis:

Pimples and cramps now shed with pelt and thews,
no dreams to fright, no visions to trouble them,
for, where the death-wish and self-knowledge fuse,
they had at last The Human L.C.M. . . .

Here the saint paused, looked modestly at the ground
and waited for their plaudits to begin.
And waited . . . There was nothing! A faint, dry sound
as first a poet buttoned on his skin.

CONQUISTADOR

I sing of the decline of Henry Clay
Who loved a white girl of uncommon size.
Although a small man in a little way,
He had in him some seed of enterprise.

Each day he caught the seven-thirty train
To work, watered his garden after tea,
Took an umbrella if it looked like rain
And was remarkably like you or me.

He had his hair cut once a fortnight, tried
Not to forget the birthday of his wife,
And might have lived unnoticed till he died
Had not ambition entered Henry's life.

He met her in the lounge of an hotel
—A most unusual place for him to go—
But there he was and there she was as well,
Sitting alone. He ordered beers for two.

She was so large a girl that when they came
He gave the waiter twice the usual tip.
She smiled without surprise, told him her name,
And as the name trembled on Henry's lip,

His parched soul, swelling like a desert root,
Broke out its delicate dream upon the air;
The mountains shook with earthquake under foot;
An angel seized him suddenly by the hair;

The sky was shrill with peril as he passed;
A hurricane crushed his senses with its din;
The wildfire crackled up his reeling mast;
The trumpet of a maelstrom sucked him in;

The desert shrivelled and burnt off his feet;
His bones and buttons an enormous snake
Vomited up; still in the shimmering heat
The pygmies showed him their forbidden lake

And then transfixed him with their poison darts;
He married six black virgins in a bunch,
Who, when they had drawn out his manly parts,
Stewed him and ate him lovingly for lunch.

Adventure opened wide its grisly jaws;
Henry looked in and knew the Hero's doom.
The huge white girl drank on without a pause
And, just at closing time, she asked him home.

The tram they took was full of Roaring Boys
Announcing the world's ruin and Judgment Day;
The sky blared with its grand orchestral voice
The Götterdämmerung of Henry Clay.

But in her quiet room they were alone.
There, towering over Henry by a head,
She stood and took her clothes off one by one,
And then she stretched herself upon the bed.

Her bulk of beauty, her stupendous grace
Challenged the lion heart in his puny dust.
Proudly his Moment looked him in the face:
He rose to meet it as a hero must;

Climbed the white mountain of unravished snow,
Planted his tiny flag upon the peak.
The smooth drifts, scarcely breathing, lay below.
She did not take the trouble to smile or speak.

And afterwards, it may have been in play,
The enormous girl rolled over and squashed him flat;
And, as she could not send him home that way,
Used him thereafter as a bedside mat.

Speaking at large, I will say this of her:
She did not spare expense to make him nice.
Tanned on both sides and neatly edged with fur,
The job would have been cheap at any price.

And when, in winter, getting out of bed,
Her large soft feet pressed warmly on the skin,
The two glass eyes would sparkle in his head,
The jaws extend their papier-mâché grin.

Good people, for the soul of Henry Clay
Offer your prayers, and view his destiny!
He was the Hero of our Time. He may
With any luck, one day, be you or me.